# Magically Sold

## *Magic Spells to SELL Your House FAST at the PRICE You Want!*

Olivia Denmark

with contributions by Walka Rusa

BANSHEE PUBLICATIONS

First published in North America
Printed by CreateSpace, An Amazon.com Company

ISBN-13: 978-1502417367
ISBN-10: 1502417367

BANSHEE PUBLICATIONS
Gilbertsville, Kentucky USA
banshee.publications@gmail.com

# Thank You

to all the kindred souls
that practice the craft.
I have learned and grown
with the help of each of you, and
I believe this book will serve its readers well.

A special thank you to
Walka Rusa and Brighid McElroy
ঙ
both wise and powerful practitioners of the art.

# Table of Contents

# Foreword

LIKE SO MANY OTHERS, I was born into the world of magic. My sisters, cousins, and I learned the craft from our grandmother, Della, and great aunt, Miami. Della was a herbalist and healer; while Miami was a midwife and empath.

They taught us that those with skill (and everyone has some level of skill) have a specialty. My sisters all tended toward the nature crafts, like Della. But my specialty seemed to be in the world of business and merchandising, especially real estate. That is how I came to develop the spells, blessings, and rituals that make up this book.

I have successfully bought and sold many houses over the last few of decades. From the East to the West, and from the North to the South, and in good markets and bad—each time I made a profit. Every house was special to me in some way, but I always knew when it was time to move on. So, I worked my magic time and again with wonderful results.

I have helped many friends and clients with the sell of their homes. In today's market, it is especially difficult to sell your home, but the spells and rituals divulged within these pages will put you ahead of the pack.

Remember, we all have power. We need to learn and practice to use it. Now is the time for you to claim your power and move on to the path of your life's journey.

ଔ   Olivia Denmark

# Opening the Circle

Hail to the East, Element of Air
Come bless us now with Light, and Love, and the breath of Life.

Hail to the South, Element of Fire
Come bless us now with Light, and Love, and Power.

Hail to the West, Element of Water
Come bless us now with the Light, and Love, and Purity.

Hail to the North, Element of Earth
Come bless us now with Light, and Love, and Security.

# The Circle is Open

# Introduction

IN TODAY'S FRANTIC WORLD, we have forgotten the wonders of nature and of magic that are around us everyday. We have forgotten that we are one with Nature and hold great personal power. Throughout time, it has been accepted that the natural world around us is alive and that spirit, mind, and body are linked. Few doubt that in order to heal a broken body, we must also heal the spirit—keeping them in balance. We also understand that all things within the cosmos is linked. And while they may appear to be solid and unrelated, they are all comprised of energy, vibrating at different frequencies. We are part of the natural world, we must be in balance with the natural world, and we have power within the natural world.

## TAKING BACK OUR POWERS

Many of us have been taught from an early age to mistrust the magic world, yet we consistently return to it instinctively. As we progress through this book, we will work on learning to trust our natural instincts and learn to utilize the personal powers we possess. We will understand that by accepting that spirit, body, and mind are aligned, and we can harness the natural energy around us. We can use magic as a way to take control of our own destinies.

For the purposes of this book, I have two goals—to get your house sold in a timely manner and at the price you want, and to help you claim (or in some cases reclaim) your own powers.

All the magic represented in this book is positive or white magic. You do not need to join a coven or secret society. You will not need expensive wands or other accessories. Most of the things you will need can be found right in your own backyard, or at the home or garden store. The real magic we will be utilizing comes from within you, the natural world around you, and the affinity of the natural with the tools you will use. By performing each spell, you are affirming what you want and what you need. Remember, you have the power within you to accomplish your goal.

## CANDLE MAGIC

Throughout time, candles have been used for spirituality and prayer. We will be using candles often in our spells. Candles represent fire, which is an important spiritual element. The flame helps us focus our minds and concentrate our energy for the spell. Candles of different colors represent different things, and we will use them accordingly.

### Color Meaning

| | |
|---|---|
| White | Purity, healing, rest, spiritual blessing |
| Green | Money, attraction, luck, business, good crops |
| Blue | Peace, harmony, kindly intentions, healing |
| Red | Love, affection, passion, bodily vigor, energy |
| Yellow | Devotion, prayer, money (gold), attraction |
| Pink | Romance, clean living |
| Purple | Power, ambition, control, command, mastery |
| Orange | Opening the way, prophetic dreaming |
| Brown | Neutrality |
| Black | Grief, freedom from evil, repulsion (to cast off) |
| Gold | Wealth and longevity, or great achievement |
| Silver | Intuition, visions and development of potential |

There are also combination colored candles used for very specific purposes, such as green and black together used to remove a money jinx. Where it is appropriate, we will be suggesting a color candle for each spell. When performing the spell, it is important to focus on the candle flame, letting your mind rest and concentrate on the golden glow. As you begin a spell, concentrate on the outcome you seek, visualizing the success, and letting the invisible natural energy around you come into you. Preparing candles for use: Candles must be cleansed and anointed (dressed). Any type of candle can be used in a ceremony.

Many who have practiced the craft for a long time insist on making their own candles. They believe it strengthens the spell, and there is less chance of the candle picking up negative energy in shipping and processing. I agree with the power of handmade candles, but for many, it is not possible to make your own. So purchased candles will do. When purchasing candles, look for ones made of all natural ingredients.

## Candle Preparation

To cleanse, simply submerge your candle in salt water and ask the God and Goddess to cleanse and consecrate it. You can certainly make up your own words. Do not rub your candle up and down. Move your hands from the top to the bottom. When removing from the water, simply move your hand from the top of the candle to the bottom, to release excess water. To anoint (or dress) a candle, rub oil in a downward motion on the candle, again asking the God and Goddess to cleanse and consecrate the candle. Any oil will do. I prefer to use an essential oil from an herb that matches the spell. Others I know, simply use a very pure olive oil.

## MOON PHASES AND MAGIC

The moon is the closest astrological body to the Earth. She controls so much of the day-to-day happenings here—the tides, axial tilt, and even moods. Each complete phase of the moon, takes exactly twenty-eight days. It is no accident that women also cycle at twenty-eight days. The moon has profound influence on us and the spells we cast. Traditionally, the full moon is the most powerful time for magic. But each phase of the moon carries special power. To find exactly the phase of the moon in your area, go to:

www.MoonConnection.com/moon_phases-calendar.phtm

- **New Moon** is the beginning of each new cycle. Generally speaking, New Moon workings can be done from the day of the new moon until three days after. However, I find that the most powerful time is right at the exact time of the new moon. This is a time of new beginnings, new ventures, love and romance, health, and job hunting.
- **Waxing Moon** starts seven days after the new moon and last for one week. This is a good time to work constructive magic, such as love, wealth, success, courage, luck, and friendship. You will see that many of the spells and blessings in this book are best done on a waxing moon.
- **Full Moon** is the most powerful time for casting. It occurs fourteen to seventeen and half days after the new moon. It is a powerful time to work spells that involve prophecy, protection, and divination. It is also a good time for healing —not only health but relationships.
- **Waning Moon** is an exceptionally good time for banishing magic. It occurs three and half, to ten days after the Full Moon. It is great for ridding oneself of addictions, illness, and negativity. Again, this time is very useful for many of the spells in this book.
- **Dark (Black) Moon** is considered to be the second most powerful time for workings. She appears ten and half to fourteen days after the Full Moon. This is the time for binding spells and exploring our dark side. Interestingly, it is also a good time for finding justice.

## NUMBER MAGIC

We will also be using the magic of numbers to achieve the outcome you desire. Numbers are all around us, especially when the goal is to sell a house—the numbers in the address, your zip code, the price, date of action, and of course your personal numbers. We all have personal numbers that represent various aspects of our life.

Finding your personal number and the number of your house

can be magically used in many ways, such as finding the best day of the month to perform a spell, or the right price for your house. When using numbers in a spell, concentrate on the attributes of that number. The true art of numerology is far too extensive of a topic to tackle in this book. We will deal with the simple numbers.

First, we will be using the Hebrew Numerological Code to allocate a number to each letter. The code is as follows:

| 1 | 2 | 3 | 4 | 5 | 6 | 7 | 8 |
|---|---|---|---|---|---|---|---|
| A | B | C | D | E | U | O | F |
| I | K | G | M | H | V | Z | P |
| J | R | L | T | N | W |   |   |
| Q | S | X |   |   |   |   |   |
| Y |   |   |   |   |   |   |   |

Now, write out your name and assign the number value to each letter, such as:

| O | L | I | V | I | A | D | E | N | M | A | R | K |
|---|---|---|---|---|---|---|---|---|---|---|---|---|
| 7 | 3 | 1 | 6 | 1 | 1 | 4 | 5 | 5 | 4 | 1 | 2 | 2 |

Add these numbers together to get 42, then add 4 + 2 = 6. My personal number is 6.

You will also want to do this for your address, such as

| 1 | 5 | 2 | H | O | L | L | O | W | W | A | Y |
|---|---|---|---|---|---|---|---|---|---|---|---|
| 1 | 5 | 2 | 5 | 7 | 3 | 3 | 7 | 6 | 6 | 1 | 1 |

So this address is 47, then add 4 + 7 = 11. This house is blessed.

Note : If your number add up to 11 or a 22, do not add the digits together to find a single digit. These numbers are master numbers and represent great magic.

### Numbers and Their Meanings

1  THE SUN: Aggression, action, ambition—symbolizes strong will, pure energy, and positivity. The number ONE is the symbolic of the sun, and thus is good for new beginnings. It

represents physical and mental action.

2  THE MOON: Balance, contrast, opposite—a good luck number meaning for TWO is about variety. It is a number that forms relationships—signifying a strong and balanced relationship. TWO reflects quiet power and tells us we have the best of both worlds. Egyptians upheld the number TWO in various symbolic amulets and rituals to represent the two-fold path of completion—knowledge and wisdom.

3  MARS: Talent, versatility, joviality—the spiritual meaning of number THREE deals with magic, intuition, fecundity, and advantage. It involves expression, versatility, and pure joy of creativity, as well as patience and belief. It is also a time identifier as in past, present, and future. THREE typically symbolizes reward and success in undertakings.

4  MERCURY: Stability, solidity, endurance—in the West, FOUR is considered good because it is grounded in stability. Some realtors love FOURs because it works well with the home. A recurrence of FOUR in your life may signify the need to get back to your roots, center yourself, or even plant yourself—FOUR represents the seasons of the year. But it also indicates a need for persistence and endurance.

5  JUPITER: Expansion, adventure, travel—FIVEs carry instability, are unpredictable, and often cause radical changes. The spiritual meaning of FIVE beckons us to appreciate the perception of chaos all around us. FIVEs are full of wild vibrations—primitive and erratic. If FIVEs continue to pop-up in your life be prepared for action and every changing relationships.

6  VENUS: Tolerant, dependable, sincere—SIX is legend. With Venus as its ruler, SIX represents harmony, balance, sincerity, love, and truth. It reveals itself in solutions in a calm, unfolding manner. The spiritual meaning of SIX also deals with enlightenment, specifically lighting our way in areas we require spiritual and mental balance and honest communications.

7 SATURN: Mystery, study, knowledge—SEVENs like THREEs deal in magical forces. It deals with the esoteric, scholarly aspects of magic. It deals with the activation of imagination and manifesting results in our lives through the use of conscious thought and awareness. Ruled by Saturn, SEVEN can represent impractical dreaming, but with a deeper understanding of the aspects of SEVEN, you can quite deftly utilize its magical vibration to your own benefit. SEVEN often signals good timing.

8 URANUS: Success, opportunity, strength—the symbolism backing EIGHT deals largely with business, success, and wealth. It is because EIGHT represents continuation, repetition, and cycles. Matters of business and wealth largely depend on cycles of fulfill their manifestation. EIGHT is in constant motion.

9 NEPTUNE: Universal influence—the spiritual meaning of number NINE brings us to the very height of vibration frequencies in this number sequences. It represents attainment, satisfaction, accomplishment, and our success to achieve an influence in our circumstance. NINE deals with intellectual power, inventiveness, influence over situations and things.

11 THE SUN: Idealism, strong vocation—the spiritual meaning of ELEVEN brings us to the level of master with a strong vocation for work and often will sacrifice their body and soul for others. It has many of the same attributes as ONE, but intensified.

22 THE UNIVERSE: Master—this number incorporates all the supreme qualities and attributes of all the other numbers. It is very blessed and carries a great responsibility with it.

## HERB AND ESSENTIAL OIL MAGIC

Sacred oils and herbs are must ingredients for most spells. Throughout time, it is believed that plants and flowers possess supernatural powers. In our daily lives, we use flowers to mark special occasions from birth to death. We use herbs to bring out our senses of taste, smell, and touch. Even our modern medical industries understand the importance of plants by using extracts to make most of their pills.

In magic, we use herbs to enhance our spells, to ward off evil, or attract money and love. We will be specific as to the kinds of herbs needed for each spell. If at all possible, grow and harvest your own herbs—your nurturing of the plants will enhance their magical power. But, if that is not possible, you may purchase your herbs from the store or on the internet. I have added an extensive herb list that correlates to house selling spells in the Appendix.

You may need a small oil, charcoal, or incense burner if you are to burn herbs for your spell. A small cauldron or bowl to mix herbs and oils may also be needed. You may want to personalize them in some way and only use them for your magic.

## GETTING STARTED

If you have done any research at all on magic, you have discovered that there are many cultural beliefs on magic. From the ancient Druids of northern Europe, the British Isles, and Ireland, to the tribes of Africa, the mystics of Asia and the Native American shamans, each group practiced magic in their own way. We will be concentrating on the basics of the western and Celtic traditions.

Each spell has a number of simple requirements:
1. When you begin and end each spell, it is important to thank the God and Goddess for intervening on your behalf.
2. Learn to concentrate. You will need to clear your mind of everything else in your life, and focus solely on the spell, visualizing your desired outcome.
3. Be very clear about your spell and desired outcome. It is never good enough to cast a spell for a better tomorrow, be specific, I want to sell this house for $299,999. Make sure you can crystallize your request in one simple sentence.
4. Pour all your soul into your magic. You must feel your magic

to gain your own power. The more vivid your picture of the outcome and the stronger your emotional attachment, the more power your magic will have.

5.  It is important that you do the physical work, as well. How can we expect the God and Goddess to help us before we do the all we can to accomplish our goal. (I have included a section on the physical aspects of selling your house in the Appendix.)

## A FINAL NOTE

The goal of this book is to provide you with simple magical spells to sell your house. Make no mistake about it—this is a stressful time for you and your loved ones. Here is a simple spell to easy stress and light the way each day.

THINGS YOU WILL NEED
- One White candle, cleansed and anointed
- Fresh grass
- Lavender
- Rose petals
- Olive oil
- Small bowl
- Incense burner

Time: Anytime you need de-stressing

1.  In the small bowl, mix the fresh grass, lavender, and rose petals with a touch of olive oil.
2.  Set the white candle in front of you, light it.
3.  Thank the powers with: *Blessed Be.*
4.  Take the incense burner and place a small amount of the herb and oil (a couple of pinches will do) in the incense burner and heat the mixture over the candle.
5.  Breathe in the fragrance of the herb mixture—in through your nose, out through your mouth. Take ten long, even breathes.

6. Focus your mind on relaxing and say: *Embrace me. Take away the burdens of the day. Embrace me. And give me light to show the way.*

7. Take two more breaths and thank the powers with: *So Mote It Be.*

8. Blow out the candle.

# Personal Cleaning Ritual

GETTING READY TO MAKE any critical decision should be preceded with a simple cleansing to clean away all the clutter of our lives. We all carry a great deal of baggage around with us, and our houses are filled with the energy clutter from all those that come and go and daily life. To make good magic, we need to clear this clutter.

THINGS YOU WILL NEED:
- Paper and pencil
- Quiet, uninterrupted time

Time: Any time, but especially powerful on the New Moon

To begin, simply turn off all outside distractions, including television, radio, computers, dishwashers, anything that is adding electromagnetic energy or noise to the environment.

1. Very clearly picture in your mind a space that is clear of all negative energy. Think about how it would feel, smell, and taste.
2. Write it down on the paper. Choose your words carefully, reflecting only positive energy, such as: *I wish to fill this space with positive energy that moves freely around me.*
3. Find a relaxing place to sit in the heart of the home—that can be any room you feel the most comfortable during your day-to-day living.
4. Hold the piece of paper in both hands, close your eyes and concentrate on breathing in and out, slowly. Allow yourself to completely relax.
5. Focus energy in your own body by concentrating on various parts of your body, starting with your hands,

then moving to your arms, neck, head, torso, abdomen, legs, and finally your feet.

6. Don't be surprised if you feel a tingling sensation on various parts of your body. Continue to concentrate on your breathing, imagining each inhalation as pure, white light, and allow the light to fill you and the space up while you exhale. Keep your focus on cleansing the space of negative energy. Notice how the space feels renewed with each breathe you take.

7. Continue the process until you feel the space is clean. When you feel complete, take a moment to express your appreciation: *Blessed Be*.

# Decision Spell

*To Sell or Not to Sell, that is the Question*
—all apologizes to Shakespeare!

IF YOU ARE LIKE MOST of us, circumstances are keeping you there and things are pulling you on to the next step. You may not be certain which force is stronger. No one ever is sure in the present. Choices may seem confusing or impossible. Certainly selling a house is a big life decision. It will decide where you are going to live or not live, where will you wake each morning, where will you close your eyes at night, kiss your children, smile at your partner, celebrate the good, and morn the bad.

Here's a ritual technique to help you to decide if you should to sell the house and if it's time to sell the house.

THINGS YOU WILL NEED:
- String—eight inches long, made of natural fiber
- Front door key
- Photograph of house

Time: Any time, but best on a Full Moon

Before any and all rituals, clear the energy around you and begin.

1. Take the key to the house—just the front door key. If there's more than one key to the front door, choose the key that you use first to open the door. Most people have a habit of using one key first. This is the key to use for this ritual. If by chance you do not have one special key, use the key to the top lock of the door.

2. Remove the key from the key ring. Tie the key to a string about eight inches long. The string should be made of a natural material, such as cotton or hemp—man-made

fibers, such as polyester do not carry the energy as accurately. Allow enough length to comfortably swing the key back and forth over a table. Tie a small knot in the other end of the string, so that it is easy to grasp.

3.  Establish the "yes" and "no" of the pendant. To do this ask an obvious question such as: *My name is* _____ (and give your real name). Wherever the pendant swings will establish that as the "yes" position. Then ask another obvious question such as: *My name is* _____ (give a false name) and that will be the "no" position.

4.  Stand above a standard height table. Place a picture of the house directly center in the table of where you are standing. Take the end string with the knot between your thumb and two middle fingers. Allow the key to swing freely over the photograph.

5.  Clear your mind of anxiety, worry, and anticipation. The pendulum will answer as it will.

6.  In a clear, strong voice, ask the question: *Should I sell my house now?*

The pendant will swing to the yes or no position. You have your answer. If you answer is yes—you have a great deal of work ahead to make sure that the house will be ready to sell on the first day of listing. If the answer is no or if you do not get a clear answer, such as the key spins in a circle—you are not done with this house. There may be things that you must experience and learn before moving on to the next step of journey.

# Blocking Obstacles in Our Path

AS YOU BEGIN TO PREPARE for the sale of your home, you will see many obstacles in your path. At any time in the process of selling you feel the obstacles are preventing movement forward, cast this spell.

THINGS YOU WILL NEED:
- One large Black candle, cleansed and anointed
- One large Green candle, cleansed and anointed
- One small Yellow candle, cleansed and anointed
- Begone or other banishing oil
- Two pieces of parchment paper and pen
- Blackberry oil or powder
- A bird feather with sharpened tip
- Small cotton/burlap bag.

Time: Any time, but best to begin on the first day of the Waning Moon

1. Take the large black candle and write with the feather (or other sharp object) directly on the candle all the objections you feel exist, such as bad marketplace, no showings—make sure to include such things as fear, worry, unknown future, etc.—be as specific as possible. NOTE: It is not important to carve into the candle, just write so that it slightly breaks the surface.
2. Dress the candle in Begone or other banishing oil
3. On the parchment, write all the same things down that you wrote on the black candle
4. For the next eight nights, at 9 pm or at midnight, set the black candle on top of the parchment and light the

candle. While the candle burns, visualize your objections and obstacles burning. Try to burn the black candle so there is only about one hour left of burning time at the end of the eighth night.

5. On night number nine, at 9 pm, light the black candle and burn the parchment in the flame. Let the candle burn until it extinguishes itself.

6. At 10 pm, write on the green candle all the reasons why it is good to follow the advice of the decision spell, such as your own misgivings about your question, mistrust of magic, etc. Write the same reasons on the second piece of parchment paper. Dress the green candle with blackberry.

7. Set the green candle on the parchment and light the candle, burning for at least one hour, concentrate on all the reasons you should follow the Decision Spell advice. Do this for four nights at 10 pm. Again, on the fourth and final night, burn the parchment in the flame of the green candle.

8. On the following night, at 10 pm, light the yellow candle to thank the powers and say: *Blessed Be, thank you for your intervention.*

9. Take the ashes and the candle stubs, place them in a small cotton/burlap bag and bury on your property on the next full moon or eleventh day of the month (which ever comes first) to keep the decision secure.

TIP: As with all spells, it is absolutely necessary that you complete the spell as described in both ingredients and time allotment, so as one does not offend the God and Goddess.

# House Blessing

THIS HOUSE HAS BEEN the focus of your life, the central point of your energies and/or your family. Soon you will be saying good-bye to it. For now, it is important that you thank this home for providing for you and your loved ones. For this spell you do not need any items, but you will need to gather all members living in the house

THINGS YOU WILL NEED:

- Everyone who lives in the home. Additional family and friends are welcome.

Time: Any time

1. Gather everyone together in the area you consider the heart of the home. This could be the living room, family room, or kitchen.
2. As a group, hold hands and say: *Welcome to all.*
3. Then as a group turn to the east. The east is the beginning, where the seed is formed. Each person needs to give thanks for the time you were in this house.
4. As a group, turn to the north, each person needs to say: *If I am ignorant of the right path, help show me. I give up whatever joy and pain has been experienced in this place.*
5. As a group, turn to the south, each person giving thanks for the light and blessings of this house.
6. As a group turn to the west, asking that the powers help each person walk forth and gather the fruit of the days' labor.
7. Turning to face each other in a circle, say: *To all four directions, to all four winds in the swirl of life that have guided me here and there, good and bad, I thank you. Stay with me as I move on. Blessed Be.*

# Smudging Ceremony

SMUDGING IS A RITUAL way to cleanse a person, place, or an object of negative energies, spirits, or influences—sort of a cosmic *out-with-the-old*. Today, most consider it a Native American tradition, but smoke has been used to cleanse and purify throughout the ages and around the world. The ceremony involves the burning of your selected herbs and/or resin and passing the object through the resulting smoke, or fanning the smoke around the person or place. The smoke is the cleansing bath. After you have thoroughly cleaned the house in a physical way, now it is time to cleanse it in a spiritual way.

THINGS YOU WILL NEED:
- Your smudging stick (or wand). You can purchase smudging sticks from a number of sources online.
- A fire-proof pan to catch the ashes
- Smudging Feather—It is traditional to use a bird's feather to brush the smoke over the person or into the space (corners and behind doors). It is important to use the underside of the feather to wash the smoke through the space. It is believed that the underside of the bird's wings that face Mother Earth as it flies offer the best connection to Nature.

Time: Any time, but best on a Waning Moon

TIP: If you prefer, you can also burn your herbs as incense by simply grinding all the herbs into a small pile. Using a heat-proof container, place a self-igniting or incense charcoal as a source of heat. If you do not have a heat-proof pan, you can use a ceramic bowl with sand at least one inch deep at the bottom—placing the charcoal on top of the sand. Light the charcoal, sprinkle about a tablespoon of smudging herb on the charcoal and fan the smoke with the feather toward the object being smudged. I personally find it hard to get the pile to burn with enough smoke to ensure a good smudging ceremony.

## THE CEREMONY FOR A SPACE

Before you begin the ceremony, say a prayer, asking the God and Goddess to grant you the spirit to complete your task. State very clearly your intentions, such as:

> *I invoke the Light of the God and Spirits*
> *to be with me and guide me.*
> *I wish to cleanse this house of negative energy, restore peace*
> *and balance, and clear the way for a prosperous sale.*

1. Begin the ceremony by greeting everyone who will participate. Stand in a circle in the first room of the house, such as an entry hall. Look into the eyes of each person. Light the smudging stick (or wand), putting out the actual fire so that the stick smolders with smoke. One person will hold a fireproof pan under the stick to catch ash as it falls. The one using the stick will hold the stick in their right hand, fanning with the bird's feather with their left.

2. Going around the circle sun-wise (clockwise or *deosil*), greet each person by fanning smoke lightly toward their heart, then start at the right side (your left) of the person's head, moving around clockwise over the head, down the left side, down across their feet and up the right side. The person needs to turn with their back facing you and repeat the smoking from their right side (your left). When completed, each person has been purified.

3. Move through the house in a sun-wise (clockwise) manner. Assume that you are at the 12 o'clock position of the house. As you enter each room, move to the left to begin your clockwise sweep. Fan smoke along the walls, into the corners, and behind doors. And don't forget to

open closets and drawers. As you move from room to room, fan smoke around the door starting at the bottom right edge (your left), up the right edge over the threshold, and down the left side before entering. In each room, say the following: *I welcome the energies within to find the gifts of healing. I welcome the energy of wisdom and blessing of the Elders. I welcome the energy and spirit of the Above. I welcome the energy of Mother Earth. I welcome the gift of purity and balance to make this place whole. I invoke the light of the God within. Make me a clear and perfect vessel to bring peace, purity, and prosperity to this place.*

4. After completing every space in the house, return to the beginning point and thank the spirits for aiding you in your endeavors by saying: *Blessed Be.*

5. Exit the house and extinguish the smudge stick.

NOTE: It is not necessary to have a group of people, but it is best to perform the ceremony with at least two people—one to hold the smudging stick and feather, and the other to hold the catching pan.

Many people like to perform the ceremony three times in a roll, especially if the space is believed to be haunted. The first pass is with white sage, or white sage and sweetgrass. The second pass through the house is with mugwort, or mugwort and sweet clover to exercise the spirits residing within. And the final pass is with sweetgrass, or sweetgrass and lavender to bring prosperity. I like to finish the ceremony by drinking wine with rosemary added—metaphysically toasting the clean house.

## MAKING YOUR OWN SMUDGING WAND

You can always purchase a smudge stick from your favorite occult store or online, but it is easy to make your own smudge stick and/or incense from scratch. Some good choices for smudging include white sage, sweet grass, rosemary, thyme, lavender, juniper, mugwort, and cedar.

There are many others. Choose herbs for its spiritual or metaphysical purpose, such as rosemary for remembrance and healing, or lavender for peace and balance. The right choice in herbs will support the intent of the spell.

It is best to grown your own herbs whenever possible, but you can also purchase herbs online and at your local nursery, garden store, grocery store, etc.

TIP: I like to cleanse any store-bought herbs before using, by rinsing them with very mild sea water.

THINGS YOU WILL NEED:
- Branches of your chosen herbs (full list in Appendix)
- Colored cotton twine or natural hemp (not polyester)
- Sharp scissors (garden clippers will do)

Time: Any time

1. Gather all your materials in one place. Your herbs should be somewhat green—not completely dried out.
2. Trim all the herbs into lengths of seven to nine inches.
3. Cut forty-seven inches (equals 11—the sun) of twine or hemp.
4. Layout your herbs in a bungle, with all stems aligned at the bottom. Pick up and hold in one hand.
5. Wrap the twine around the bottom tips of the bundle a couple of times to secure them together. Then bind the bundle by wrapping in a cross-cross pattern to form a stick. Once you reach the top of your bundle, continue wrapping until you are back on the bottom. Tie a knot to secure the bundle and trim off excess twine or jute.
6. Let the smudge stick dry for a week. The bundle should be dry enough to burn, but not so dry as to burst into flame.

TIP: My personal favorite combination for a house cleaning is:
- 1/3 white sage to drive out negative energy
- 1/3 lavender to restore balance and create a peaceful atmosphere
- 1/3 juniper to provide protection

For a house selling ceremony, I like to throw in sweet clover to bring in prosperity. If the house is haunted, I use mugwort with sage alone.

# Burying a St. Joseph Statue

YOU DO NOT NEED TO be Catholic or even traditional Christian, to follow the tradition of burying a St. Joseph statue. The tradition of burying a St. Joseph statute to ensure a house will have a quick sale is an old one. The practice began in Europe hundreds of years ago (A.D. 1515-1582), when Sister Teresa of Avila and the nuns of her cloister convent needed to expand their land. As part of their prayers to St. Joseph, they buried medals of him in the ground. After a very short time, they found their prayers had been answered, when they were endowed with additional lands. No one seems to know when the practice went from burying medals to statues or from acquiring to selling.

THINGS YOU WILL NEED:
- Statue of St. Joseph (or make your own)
- Shovel or spade
- Prayer to St. Joseph

Time: Any time, but Sundays have worked best for me

1. Choose a position of honor at the front of the home. Having an emotional connection to the spot is helpful, such as this is the place you greet your guests, or it is the place where you first stood and looked at the house before you bought it. If there is no place in particular, burying the statue near the "For Sale" sign is a good idea. I have always buried my St. Joseph statue in the dead center of the front yard, and have moved the "For Sale" sign to near the statue. If you live in a townhouse or condominium, use a large plant pot.

2. Dig a hole that is at least three inches deeper than the height of your statue.
3. Place your St. Joseph statue in the hole, upside down, with St. Joseph facing the house (or else the house across the street or next door may sale faster than yours).
4. Fill in the dirt, and recite the following prayer to St. Joseph:

*O, Saint Joseph,*
*I beset you to help me now as you have helped many others in the matter of housing.*
*I endeavor to sell this house/property quickly, easily, and profitably.*
*I petition you to grant my wish by bringing me a buyer, who is good and honest for the sake of this community, who is qualified and compliant for the sake of the sale.*
*And let nothing impede the rapid conclusion of the sale.*
*O, Saint Joseph,*
*I beg you will do this for me out of the goodness in your heart and in your own good time.*
*My need is great, so I ask that you hurry on my behalf.*
*Then, Saint Joseph, I swear that I will redeem you and you will receive my gratitude and a place of honor in my new home.*
*Amen (or Blessed Be)*

5. It is worthwhile to make this prayer a daily ritual, while the house is on the market.
6. After the house is sold, retrieve the statue of St. Joseph and put it in a place of honor in your new home.

## MAKE A SAINT JOSEPH STATUE

Inexpensive St. Joseph statues are readily available from religious supply shops or online, but there are those that believe a handmade St. Joseph carries more power.

THINGS YOU WILL NEED:
- Picture of St. Joseph
- Glue
- Small plastic bottle
- Scissors
- Fabric (crafting felt or cotton muslin work nicely)
- Cotton batting (wadding for our British friends)
- Needle and Thread

SIMPLE PLASTIC BOTTLE STATUE:
1. Purchase a photo of St. Joseph or print one online.
2. Cut out just the image of St. Joseph.
3. Clean the small plastic bottle. It is best to do this in pure water or spring water directly from nature. Some believe that holy water is best.
4. Glue image to one side of the plastic bottle.
5. Follow the ceremony instructions from before.

CLOTH DOLL STATUE:
1. Purchase a photo of St. Joseph or print one from online.
2. Cut out just the image of St. Joseph.
3. Cut two (2) identical person-shaped figures from the cloth. (See pattern on following page.)
4. Sew the two figures together by stitching around the edge of the figures with right sides together, leaving the top of the head open.
5. Turn the cloth doll inside out, so that the stitching is on the inside. You may need to clip around curved seamlines to get it to open completely up.
6. Stuff the cloth doll with the batting, you may need to use a pencil to get the batting into the legs and arms. Then stitch close the top of the head.
7. Cut out the face of St. Joseph from your photo. Either glue or stitch the face to one side of the head.

Cut two identical pieces from fabric. It is best to use a natural fabric, such as 100% cotton, or 100% hemp. Use a quarter-inch seam allowance when sewing.

The traditionally the statue is buried upside down, so as to make St. Joseph uncomfortable, so that he will facilitate a quick sale and be retrieved from the ground.

# Casting Out Ghosts

A PROBLEMATIC GHOST or spirit can be a real deterrent to the sale of your house. It is best to cast those pesky spirits out before potential buyers come knocking.

There are a number of logistical and legal issues involving haunted houses. See page ??? for more specifics on how having a haunted house impacts you as the house-seller. But if you have a ghost or spirit, there are a number of simply things to try to rid the property of the ghosts and/or spirits. You may want to simply speak with the entity, asking that they move on. You can also paint your door red. It is believed that ghosts are scared of the color red and they will not enter. Of course, I worry that if they are already in the house, they won't leave through a red door. For more severe hauntings, here is a ritual to help you, help them to pass over.

THINGS YOU WILL NEED:
- Sea water
- Fennel (a few tablespoons will do)
- Oats (a few tablespoons will do)
- Pine needles (a handful)
- White Sage (a few tablespoons will do)
- Teapot
- Strainer
- Bowl
- Bell

Time: It would be best to perform this ceremony on a Dark Moon, especially if you have a particularly nasty ghost.

1. Heat the sea water to a boil in your teapot. (If you do not have access to actual sea water, you can make your own using purified water and sea salt).

2. Mix the herbs—fennel representing fire, oats representing earth, pine representing air, and sage representing wisdom.
3. Steep the herbs with the sea water to make a strong tea.
4. Strain out the herbs (but do not throw them away). Pour the tea into the bowl.
5. Open the windows and doors of the house.
6. Taking the tea and the bell, move through your house and each room in a counter-clockwise manner (or widdershins). Sprinkle a few drops of the tea at each corner, window and door, saying:

   *Your time has come, and you must leave,*
   *You are welcome here, or with me,*
   *Where light dwells, darkness flees*
   *Follow the light, and take your leave.*

7. After each saying, ring the bell three times.
8. After you have completed the inside of the house, close all the windows.
9. Taking the herbs left from the house, the tea and the bell, repeat the ceremony moving around the outside of your house, sprinkling the tea, spread the herbs, and repeat the verse, and ring the bell three times.
10. Finish the ceremony with: *Blessed Be.*

You should feel an immediate lightness to the house. You may want to follow this up with a House Cleansing or Smudging Ceremony. However, if the ghost and spirit has not moved on, you may want to call in a professional.

Of course, many people like to have some company around and don't mind a ghost or spirit roaming around. Just follow the legalities, and inform potential buyers of the presence of an eternal resident.

# Cleaning and Clutter Magic

THE PROCESS OF CLEANING and removing clutter from your home in preparation for selling is powerful magic all by itself. Getting rid of all the things that don't fit, are worn out, out-of-date, or just plain dirty helps us re-align ourselves with nature.

When selling a house, you want to remove everything that is in the way, creating a balanced space. As you move through, you must decide what is enhancing the energy of the space, and what is taking energy away. It is important that the energy you are giving off is balanced with the house, as well.

THINGS YOU WILL NEED:
- One bright Red candle, cleansed and anointed
- Incense made of equal parts of any three of the following:
    Jasmine: luck
    Blueberry: keeps unwanted influences away
    Cinnamon: success, healing, psychic powers
    Frankincense: stimulate positive energies
    Clove: dispel negativity, attracts money
    Patchouli: money and attraction
    Pine: strength and reverse negative energies
    Ginseng Root: keeps wicked spirits away
    Rue: restores health
- Incense burner
- Sea salt
- Small bowl
- Glass of pure (not distilled) cold water

Time: Any time, but best on the Waning Moon

1. Pour sea salt into bowl and sit it on left-hand side of table or altar.
2. Sit red candle in center of table or altar. Light the candle.
3. Place the incense burner and incense on right-hand side of table or alter. Light the incense.
4. Place the glass of water directly in front of you.
5. Sit before the table or altar and take three deep, calming breathes (in through your nose, out through you mouth).
6. Then say: *I call on the spirits to give me the energy the task before me.*
7. Take a pinch of the sea salt from the bowl and sprinkle around the candle base, saying: *Give me Strength from the Sacred Earth.*
8. Pass you hand over the candle flame (do not burn yourself) saying: *Give me Strength from the Sacred Fire.*
9. Pass your hand through the smoke of the incense, saying: *Give me Strength from the Sacred Air.*
10. Take the glass of water and drink all of it. Then say: *Give me Strength from the Sacred Water.*
11. Thank the powers by saying: *Blessed Be.*

Get up and immediately begin the task of setting the house to rights for a sale.

# Choosing A Realtor Or Not!

CHOOSING A REALTOR or choosing to sell it yourself is a hard decision. There are so many things that will need to be done to present your house to the marketplace. And deciding who will best represent you and the house is critical to the success. Here is a simple spell to help you make the decision.

THINGS YOU WILL NEED:
- Bowl of water (sea water/salt water, preferably)
- Stick or twig (a small twig from your yard will work, or a sprig of rosemary is also nice). Make sure the stick is smaller than the diameter of the bowl. Make sure to define one end of the stick as the point.
- A green candle, cleansed and anointed
- Business cards from the realtors you are considering (make sure you have narrowed it down to no more than four names).
- If you are considering acting as your own agent, you will need three business-size cards (2 inches x 3.5 inches), with your name on them.

Time: Best on the New Moon or the Waxing Moon

1. Gather three copies of each business card you are considering.
2. Set the bowl of water in the middle of the table.
3. Place the business cards (and your card) around the bowl face down. Make sure to spread them randomly so that no two identical cards are together.
4. Place the unlit green candle above the bowl of water at the 12 o'clock position.

5.  Sit before the bowl with your hands on your knees with your palms facing up to the sky.
6.  Slowly breathe in through your nose and out through your mouth, calming yourself and centering your thoughts
7.  Once you are calm and ready to proceed, light the candle and say: *With this fire, fulfill my desire.*
8.  Thinking of the decision you have to make, place the stick (or twig) in the water, so that it floats on top. With your thumb and forefinger of your right hand, spin the stick clock-wise (deosil). Say the following:
    *I need to decide and I request your advice,*
    *Sent it once, send it twice.*
    *Please show me the one*
    *Who can make the sale.*
9.  Continue to concentrate as the stick continues to spin in the water. Once the water stops moving the stick, it should point to one of the cards. Turn it over and you have your answer.
10. Finish the ceremony by thanking the spirits and glowing out the candle. *Blessed Be. Thank you for your wisdom.*

NOTE: This is a wonderful decision spell and can be used for any major decision. You can substitute notes of the various options before you for the business cards.

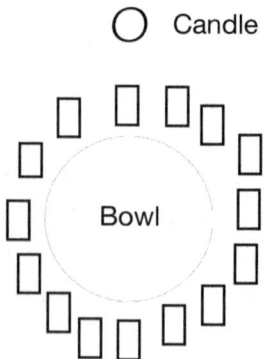

○ Candle

Bowl

# Setting the Price

PRICING THE HOUSE is a huge undertaking and froth with anxiety. Do you own research on what houses in your area are selling for—make sure to look at the size, number of bedrooms and baths, updates, location, and condition. Also, follow your realtors advice, they should know the local market. In the end, the pricing decision is up to you, so make sure to include your sacred personal number and the number of your house. See pages ??? to establish those numbers. My personal number is 6, so I always end my pricing with a 6, instead of a 5 or 9, which is more traditional. The last house I sold, had a numerology number of 9, so I used 996 as the last numbers in my pricing. After setting your price, bless it with the following:

THINGS YOU WILL NEED:
- Picture of the house as it will appear on the forth-coming sell sheet, print and web advertising, and realtor catalog.
- Small paintbrush
- Green ink or water color
- Green candle, cleansed and anointed
- Incense, use herbs with prosperity properties

Time: Any time, but best on a Waxing Moon

1. Sit the candle in front of you on your altar or on a table.
2. Place the incense to the right of the handle. Lit only the incense.
3. Take the picture of the house. Using the green ink, write: SOLD FOR $ (put in your price) and add the date of the ritual.
4. Lay the photo in front of the candle and light the candle.
5. Concentrate on selling the house and what that will mean to you. Take deep breaths and relax.

6. When you feel the time is right, clap three times, saying the price as you clap.
7. Extinguish the candle by wetting your fingers and pinching out the flame—DO NOT BLOW IT OUT (or you will be blowing away the price).
8. Finish the ceremony with: *Blessed Be, Thank you for your intervention on my behalf.*
9. Put the picture in a secure place in the house.

You may repeat this ceremony as many times as you wish to aid in your sale.

## Make a Lucky Talisman

Create a simple talisman to carry with you during the process of selling your home. In this case, the talisman is specifically design to enhance the opportunities of money coming your way.

THINGS YOU WILL NEED:
- 3 Chinese coins
- Red ribbon

1. Tie the three Chinese coins in the middle red ribbon.
2. Hold each end of ribbon, so that the coins dangle in the center.
3. Starting at the true east of your house, walk abound the house in a clock-wise direction, three times.
4. Saying the price you want for the house as you move.
5. Place the ribbon and coins in the back of your check book or accounts book.

# Bring Success to the Sell

IT IS IMPORTANT THAT you cast a spell for success, because in reality you are beginning a business venture. This spell should only be worked after you have made the decision to use a realtor or to represent yourself and after you have set an asking price.

THINGS YOU WILL NEED:

- A small quantity of dry apple wood. It is important that you do not purchase this apple wood. You must cut it yourself—preferably from your own property, or that of a loved one—remember that before you cut or gather the wood, ask for its blessing before just taking it, or your must barter another living thing, or your own personal labor to get it. It is best to gather the wood on a full moon, or at the beginning of the waxing cycle.
- Sea water, brine, or holy water (preferably salted holy water)
- Essential oil of heather or lavender.
- A place to burn the wood, such as a fireplace, fire pit, or oil burner

Time: This spell takes an entire lunar cycle. You can begin at any time, but I suggest you begin on a Waxing Moon and end on a Waxing Moon to achieve the highest power for money. This spell must be continued for twenty-eight days of a lunar month cycle. So begin the spell on the first night of the Waxing Moon.

1. Gather your apple wood and ask permission and blessing as you do by saying: *I ask for this gift from the Earth to aid me in my success.*

2. Soak the apple wood in the sea water for the twenty-eight days of the lunar cycle.

3. On the Waxing Moon, retrieve the wood from the sea water. Shake off or towel dry the wood as much as possible. Sprinkle the essential oil over the wood liberally.

4. Place the wood in your burner, and set a fire.

5. As the wood begins to burn, say the following three times:

     *May this gift from the wood, and gift from the sea, bring luck to my plans and desires and blossom like the flame of the apple bough. May this gift from the wood and gift from the sea bring success and wisdom to me (and name of agent).*

6. Make sure to concentrate on the sell of the house and the price you wish, and the your agent.

7. Finish the ceremony by bowing to the flames with your hands clasped and thank the powers for their intervention on your behalf. *Blessed Be. Thank you for hearing my prayers.*

# Initial House Selling Spell

HOUSES HAVE A SPIRIT and energy all their own. It is said that buyers will make their decision within seconds on whether the house is right for them. The spirit of the house has a lot to do with how buyers view it—the house must be open to new owners.

THINGS YOU WILL NEED:
- A nice jar with a good lid or stopper
- Quartz crystal shards, enough to fill the jar

Time: Any time, but best on a Full Moon

1. Fill the jar with quartz crystal shards.
2. Leaving the lid or stopper off, take the jar onto the front porch, face the door, and holding the jar out with both hands, say:
   *I am here to release this house.*
   *I take back my time, memories, energy, and love.*
   *I release you house, setting us both free to move on.*
3. Go into the house, the room that you consider the center of the house, and repeat the process. Do this in every room. Don't forget the basement or the attic (if you lived in it).
4. Seal the jar closed.
5. Go back into the room that is the center and say:
   *I thank you, house*
   *I wish you well with new owners and a new life.*
   *I wish us both good fortune.*
   *Blessed Be.*

When you get to your new home, open the jar. Then you can discard the crystals and jar.

# Website Blessing & Talisman

GETTING THE WORD OUT that your house is on the market is critical to a successful sale. You want to reach as many people as humanly and magically possible. In today's world, that means that you will need to have a great web presence to accomplish your goal. Of course, other marketing tactics will also be used, including classified ads, catalogs of homes, sell-sheets, and realtor networks. Begin by making a marketing success charm bag.

THINGS YOU WILL NEED:
- Make or buy a small draw-string bag, about two to four inches deep. It should be of a natural fiber such as cotton, wool, silk, or burlap.
- Equal parts of:
    Bayberry: attracts money
    Red clover: success, money and protection
    Comfrey: safety and healing
    Dragon's Blood: enticement and potency
    Mandrake Root: money and health
    Five to six Tulip petals: protection
- Pen
- Small picture of the house
- One Gold candle, cleansed and anointed
- Sandlewood incense and incense burner
- Sea salt
- Pure, spring water

Time: Any time, best on the success of the Waxing Moon

1. Use the pen to inscribe the runes* of Dagaz, Fehu and Tiwaz on the mandrake root.

2. On the back of the photo, write the price you want to receive for the house.
3. On a Wednesday or Thursday of the Waxing Moon, place all the elements in the bag.
4. Place the candle and incense on your table or altar. Light both.
5. With your witching hand (your dominant hand), use your index finger to draw a pentacle between the candle and incense. Place the bag directly on over of the pentacle.
6. Sprinkle a little salt on the bag, and say: *I consecrate this talisman with Earth.*
7. Pass the bag through the smoke of the incense and say: *I consecrate this talisman with Air.*
8. Pass the bag through the flame (don't sit the bag on fire) and say: *I consecrate this talisman with Fire.*
9. Sit the bag back down on the pentacle, and sprinkle some of the spring water on it, saying: *I consecrate this talisman with Water.*
10. Place both hands over the bag, visualizing light pouring into the talisman and say: *I charge this talisman by the elemental powers of Earth, Air, Fire and Water.*

Each day, open the websites that contain your house for sale information. Hold the talisman high in your right hand and ask that internet users be drawn to the web page and call the realtor. Keep the talisman by your computer. Do the same with catalogs and advertisements for the house.

You might also want to make a second talisman and give it to the realtor to bring him/her luck in the sale of the house.

*The RUNES: Runes are letters in a family of ancient alphabets known as runic alphabets. Runes were used as a method of communication across Scandinavia and in other Germanic nations from around the 3rd century CE (or AD) to around the 13th century, when they were displaced by the Roman alphabet.

Runes are also used as a tool for divination, since these individuals believe that runes have mysterious powers.

 DAGAZ—The Rune of Transformation. Its characteristics include a new dawn or major change of direction. It also signifies achievement and prosperity—a successful conclusion to a passage.

 FEHU—The Rune of Wealth and Fulfillment. Its characteristics include realized ambition. Good health, wealth, and love fulfilled. It also signifies good fortune.

 TIWAZ—The Warrior's Rune. Its characteristics include tactical genius, courage, bravery, dedication and daring. Good negotiating and legislative ability follows it.

# Buyer Attraction Spell

IT IS IMPORTANT TO GET as many potential buyers into your house for viewing as possible. The more visitors, the more potential you have for receiving top dollar at closing. Here is a magic potion and spell to bring buyers to your door.

THINGS YOU WILL NEED:
- A small jar with a lid
- Small bowl for mixing
- Equal parts:
  Basil: wealth and protection
  Alfalfa: prosperity and protection against financial misfortune
  Caraway: anti-theft, lust, and memory
  Buckwheat: money and guard against poverty

Time: New Moon

1. Mix all the herbs in the bowl, while saying:
   *Money comes and money grows,*
   *Quickly in the buyers flow*
   *Fill my hands with lots of offers*
   *So that I may refill by coffers*
   *So Mote It Be!*
2. Pour the mixture into the jar and put on the lid.
3. Each morning when there is a showing or open house, rub a small amount of the powdery mixture on your front door knob. If you have a front gate that visitors must enter, rub some of the mixture on the gate handle, as well.

# Open House/ Showing Blessing

EVERY HOUSE, AND WE mean every house, has imperfections, just as people have imperfection. Since you have lived in the house, you probably know them all. In my opinion, that is what gives a house character. But when you are trying to sell a house, you don't want potential buyers to see those imperfections. Here is a simple spell to provide a little make-up for your open house or house viewing. This is especially important to do if you have buyers coming back for a second or third look at the house.

THINGS YOU WILL NEED:
- One Red candle, cleansed and anointed
- One small Rose Quartz crystal (small enough to fit in bottle)
- Six rose petals
- Witch hazel
- Small bottle, with lid or stopper
- Photograph or sell-sheet of the house

Time: Best on the night before the showing, but especially powerful on a Full Moon

1. Set the red candle on your table or altar. Light it.
2. Pour a small amount of witch hazel in the bottle, and put the lid or stopper back on.
3. Concentrate on all the wonderful things about the house—the things you believe others will love about it.
4. When you feel relaxed and ready to proceed, take out the photo (or sell-sheet) of the house and place flat on the table or altar between you and the candle.
5. Take the rose quartz crystal and rub it lightly over the

picture saying:

> *Stone of Beauty, Stone of Love*
> *Erase all imperfection as I rub*
> *Bring in buyers to the place I see*
> *As I will so mote it be!*

6. Open the bottle with the witch hazel, and place the quartz crystal inside, and put the lid or stopper back on.

7. Take the rose and rub them lightly over the picture saying:

> *Petal of Beauty, Petal of Love*
> *Erase all imperfection as I rub*
> *Bring in buyers to the place I see*
> *As I will so mote it be!*

8. Open the bottle with the witch hazel and quartz crystal, and place the rose petals inside. Replace the lid or stopper and shake three times, saying:

> *In the eye of the buyer will only be,*
> *The perfect house they want to see.*

9. Sprinkle a few drops of the witch hazel mixture on the welcome mat or front step just prior to open house or showing.

TIP: I also like to place a few drops around the "For Sale" sign—especially if you have a sell-sheet dispenser on it.

Remember to place yellow flowers in a vase near the front door. On the day of the open house or showing. Also, place lemons in a bowl in the kitchen—make sure one lemon is cut in half on the plate or cutting board.

MOST IMPORTANT: Make sure each visitor arrives and leaves through the front door. A buyer that comes in the front door and exits through the back door, may take prosperity with them.

TIP: Put blueberries under the doormat of the door visitors will enter. It will keep away undesirables.

# Sweep Out Negativity

AFTER ANY OPEN HOUSE or day of house showing, there is bound to be some negative energies brought in by those viewing the house. There are people coming through the door that are depressed, stressed-out about house-hunting, and those that just like to dump their bad *ju-ju* on someone else.

After each showing, I like to perform a little besom ritual to sweep all the negativity away. A besom is simply a broom. A more traditional Wicca broom would be made from birch, heather, or broom twigs. It is said that the gypsies were the first to discover the magic of the besom, and use it in many ceremonies.

THINGS YOU WILL NEED:
- A besom, or a traditional broom will work
- Incense—sandlewood or lavender are favorites

Time: Anytime

1. Sweep all the floors in your house, moving the besom backwards— pushing the energy behind you.
2. As you sweep, say the following:
   *All negativity stuck in here*
   *Be swept away, I have no fear.*
   *Rise and leave this space*
   *Negativity not welcome in this space.*
3. Make sure to sweep all the dust out the back door, else you may be sweeping away an offer coming in the front.
4. After you are through, light the incense to sweeten the air with positivity.

# House Selling Spell Again!

SO, THE HOUSE HAS BEEN on the market for a while. There has been some showings, but still no offers. It's time to get serious about doubling your efforts to sell this house. You need to break the impasse of this house and the potential buyers.

THINGS YOU WILL NEED:
- Four Frankincense incense sticks
- Incense stick holders
- Sell-sheet for your house
- House key
- Spring water (not tap water, unless you have a well)
- Bowl of water

Time: Full Moon

1. Place the sell-sheet for your house face up in the center of your table or altar.
2. On top of the sell-sheet, place the four incense sticks in their holders—one at the top center, one at the bottom center, on to the center left and one to the center right.
3. Place the key in the center of the sell-sheet.
4. Pour the spring water into the bowl and sit it to the side.
5. Light the incense, starting with the one at the top of the sheet, then the one on right, bottom and finally left. While lighting the incense, say: *May the winds of change, blow in an offer on this house.*
6. Take the incense set in the center of the top, and pass it around the top of the key in a clock-wise (doesil) circle three times saying: *I remove the wall, Blow in an offer on this house.*

7. Plunge the burning incense into the spring water.
8. Take the incense on the right side of the sell-sheet and repeat the process. Remember, three circles, clock-wise, repeating the chant.
9. Take the incense at the bottom of the sell-sheet and repeat the process.
10. Take the incense at the left of the sell-sheet and repeat the process.
11. After you have extinguished all four incense sticks, pick up the bowl and hold it over the key, saying:
    *May the winds of change,*
    *Blow away all barriers to an offer*
    *May the offer be true and strong.*
    *So Shall It be.*

This spell can be cast over and over, as necessary. If you do not have time to await the Full Moon, the Waxing Moon is good, as well.

# Spell for Successful Offer

THE BEST WORDS A REALTOR can say to you is: "I have a good offer in hand." Making sure you are getting a number of quality offers is very important. You want to attract buyers that are already pre-qualified for whatever financing they are arranging. Or better yet, a cash offer. In the end, you want a buyer that will follow through to closing. This spell is all about bringing successful offers to you.

THINGS YOU WILL NEED:
- One Green candle, cleansed and anointed. Candle can be a taper or votive size.
- One Purple candle, cleansed and anointed. Candle can be a taper or votive size.
- An extra house key
- Gold ribbon or gold chain (you will be wearing this as a necklace, so make sure it is something you are comfortable with to wear pretty constantly).

Time: Anytime

1. Go into the room you consider the center of the house.
2. Place the green candle on one side of the room. Do not light it yet.
3. Place the purple candle on the opposite side of the room, but make sure there are not obstructions between the two candles. Light it.
4. Place the house key on the ribbon or chain.
5. Holding the ribbon (or chain), dangling from your left hand, pick up the purple candle while the flame is burning.

6.  In a straight line, walk to the green candle across the room, saying: *I move forth without doubt or fear. Bring successful house offers near.*

7.  Light the green candle from the flame of the purple candle. Sit the purple candle down beside the green candle. Place the house key on the ribbon between the two candles.

8.  Mediate on the flames and seeing the offers for the price you want in the light.

9.  Do not blow out the candles. Let them burn down on their own.

10. When they candles have extinguished themselves, place the ribbon or chain with the house key around you neck. Do not take it off until you have a signed contract.

# Protection Against Bad Buyers

FINAL CONTRACTS ARE FULL of legalize. Even most lawyers do not understand everything that is in them. You will want to bless the contract to make sure that what you understand the contract to be is exactly what is in that contract. Make sure that you get copies of all the legal offer papers. You want to make sure that the people making the offer are not out to steal from you. Here is a little potion to help ward off fraudulent people.

THINGS YOU WILL NEED:
- Equal parts:
  Galangal
  Turmeric (powered root)
  Poppy seeds
- Small bowl
- Incense burner
- Charcoals for the burner
- Copy of the offer papers
- Small pouch made of black cloth (100% cotton or silk)

Time: Any time, but best on the Waning Moon

1. Place the incense burner on your table or altar. Make sure that it will not scar or burn your table or altar when lit.
2. Add the charcoal and lit.
3. Mix the herbs together in the bowl.
4. Put the herb mixture into the incense burner and let them burn to ash.
5. As the incense burner smokes, pass the offer papers through the smoke, saying the following three times: *Let this contract be true and valid.*

6. When the ashes cool. Gather the ashes into the black pouch, and say: *Blessed Be.*
7. Place the pouch on top of the offer papers and let them sit.
8. On the day of the closing, make sure to put the pouch in your left pocket and carry it with you.

If the offer is fraudulent or the buyers untrustworthy, the offer will be withdrawn. If there is something wrong with the legal papers or financing, it will show itself prior to the closing.

TIP: I prefer a silk pouch for this particular spell. Silk is a natural barrier and will help keep evil out.

# Home Inspection Invisibility Spell

ONCE YOU HAVE A GOOD offer on the house you want to sell, you will need to officially accept that offer. Then things start to move very quickly (at least in most cases), so you will want to make sure that the house inspection goes as you want. Remember, every house—and I do mean every house—has something not quite right. After all, only the divine can create perfection. As the seller, you want to minimize the problems that a home inspector might find. Here is a recipe for an invisibility powder that will help the inspector overlook issues with the house that will cost you money.

THINGS YOU WILL NEED:
- Mixture
    One part bracken (dried)
    One part poppy seed
    One part myrrh
    One part marjoram (dried)
    Two parts dill weed (fresh from the garden)
    Two parts white oak bark (ground)
    Almond extract
- Pestle and mortar (or something else to grind the herbs)
- Spring water
- Ceramic or glass bowl (that can go into the oven)
- Small jar
- Spray bottle
- Oven, set at 200°F (95°C)

Time: Anytime

1. Grind all the herbal ingredients together so they are mixed well. I like to do this is my pestle and mortar.
2. Add eleven drops of almond extract to make the herb mixture moist and slightly pasty in texture.
3. Coat the inside of ceramic (or glass) bowl. Spread it thinly.
4. Place the bowl in the oven, so that the mixture can dried and slightly brown. Time will depend on how much you are making. Watch it closely.
5. Remove all the mixture from the bowl, and regrind. (Note I like to do this by hand with a pestle and mortar). While it is grinding, say:

   *Things seen, and things not seen,*
   *Let the inspector only see*
   *The things I deem to be seen*
   *So mote it be.*

6. Place the finely ground powder in a glass for storage.
7. Prior to any inspection, take a little of the powder and rub on things you don't want the inspector to find. Or mix the powder with spring water and use on a spray for the same purpose.

# Appraisal Money Spell

IF YOU HAPPEN TO BE one of the lucky ones, your buyers are paying cash and will not need to go through a bank or mortgage company for approval. However, most buyers finance their real estate purchases. Which means you will most likely have to go through the appraisal process. This ensures that the company making the loan for the house will get their money's worth, if the future buyer defaults on the loan. That's all very technical, but basically, you want the house to appraise for higher than the sell price.

THINGS YOU WILL NEED:
- One large Gold candle, cleansed and anointed
- Three small Green candles (can be votive), cleansed and anointed
- A quill or bird feather
- Picture of the house
- Red ribbon
- Fire-proof bowl or incense burner

Time: Anytime, but best on Waxing or Full Moon

1. Place the gold candle at the 12 o'clock position on your table or altar.
2. Place the green candles in a straight line horizontally (from the 9 o'clock position to the center, to the 3 o'clock position) in front of the gold candle (between you and the gold candle).
3. Place the picture of the house in front of the green candles.
4. Light each candle, beginning with the gold, then the three green candles—from left to right.
5. As the candles burn, meditate on the appraisal and

the figure you would like to see as the appraised value. Picture the appraiser walking through the house and neighborhood. Picture him/her writing down the number you want.

6. Take your quill and dip it into the melted wax of the first green candle on the right. Then write the appraisal value on the house photo in wax. Make the numbers large to fill the space horizontally.

7. Now tip the quill into the melted wax of the middle green candle, and do the same.

8. Finally, dip your quill in the melted wax of the green candle on the left, and write the value again on the house photo.

9. Now roll the house photo up and tie it with the red ribbon.

10. Hold the photo above the gold candle in the smoke, and say:

    *May the appraiser only see beauty.*
    *May the appraiser only see value.*
    *May the appraiser only see (give the amount).*

11. Light one end of the photo (scroll) in the gold candle flame and let it burn (make sure to place it in the fireproof bowl, or incense burner). As it burns, say: *So Mote It Be!*

12. Collect the ashes and spread them in front of your front door. If you live in an apartment or condo, place the ashes in a plant near the front door.

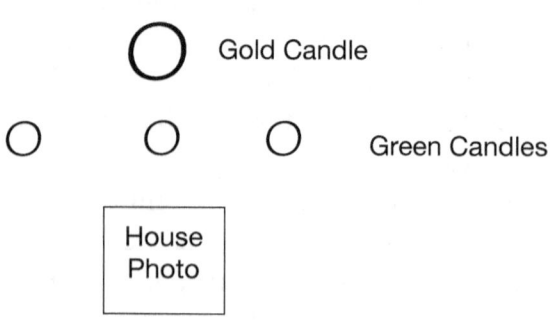

Gold Candle

Green Candles

House Photo

# Successful Closing Blessing

YOU ARE FINALLY AT the end of this journey called selling your house. The closing of the contract is packed full of energy. There are so many moving parts that must come together on a specific day in a specific place. It is a stressful time for both the seller and the buyer. Everyone is nervous that something is not going to go correctly. This blessing brings in all the elements to ensure a successful closing for both parties.

THINGS YOU WILL NEED:
- Fresh flowers, preferably from your own garden or houseplants.
- Cinnamon incense
- Incense burner
- Gold candle, cleansed and anointed
- Rose Water—purchased, or make your own from rain water or spring water, and rose petals
- Small bowl
- Compass to know true north.
- Contract or closing papers (a copy will do)

Time: Best the night before closing, especially in a Waxing or Full Moon phase.

1. Pour the rose water into the bowl.
2. Place the ingredients on a table or altar in the following order.
   Flowers, representing earth, to the North.
   Incense, representing air, to the East.
   Candle, representing fire, to the South.
   Bowl, representing water, to the West.

3. Place the contract or a copy of the contract in the center of all the other elements.

4. Light the candle and incense, and say:
   *I evoke the elements of Earth, Air, Fire and Water.*
   *I beseech you to aid me in a successful contract.*

5. Meditate before the table/altar. Visualize signing the papers, Visualize handling over the keys to the new owners. Visualize receiving the check. Visualize the next things you will do after the closing.

6. Close with: *Blessed Be.*

# Casting for New Home

WE HAVE BEEN CONCENTRATING on selling your house, but where are you going to live next? Usually, it is not just a matter of finding the house you want. We often face other types of hurdles, such as tight finances, lag time between selling your house and moving, etc.

One of the first orders of business is to decide what you want and where you want it. From personal experience, I find it helpful to take a long cleansing bath. Then I gather everyone who will reside in the new place together to decide what we want. We talk about size, cost, location, amenities, outdoor space, neighbors, etc. I usually burn a soothing incense while we meet—patchouli is good due to its money and attraction properties. Together, we write down all the items that are important to us on a parchment. I then take this parchment and cast my spell.

THINGS YOU WILL NEED:
- The parchment you prepared with the rest of the household. This will be your petition.
- Clover
- Patchouli oil
- Orange candle, cleansed and anointed
- Pen

Time: New Moon is best

1. At your altar or table, place the orange candle in the center and light it.
2. Take the parchment (petition), lay it on the altar in front of you, face up.
3. Place a small amount of clover on the paper. Then fold the paper down one-third beginning at the top of the page. Now fold the bottom of the page up one-third. Take

the left side and fold it in one-third. Now, take the right side and fold it in one-third. The clover should be sealed inside.

4. Dip the tip of your wand or wand finger (index finger of your dominant hand) in the patchouli oil, and draw the shape of a house on the parchment petition.
5. Take your pen and write your name and the names of everyone in the household inside the house.
6. Place the petition under the burning candle. Let the candle burn down completely.
7. Begin your house hunt. Keep the petition with you at all times.

You will quickly find the home that will meet your needs and desires.

# Blessing of the Keys

I ALWAYS LIKE TO BLESS the keys of the house I just sold before handing them over to the new owners. For me, it is an act of completion. I also bless the keys to any new place I have selected to live. The goal is that all parties are happy with their decisions and will live happily in their new homes. This is a pretty simple ceremony and is generally a good blessing.

THINGS YOU WILL NEED:
- Keys to the house
- 1 White candle, cleansed and anointed
- Pen, needle or feather to scribe onto the candle

Time: Anytime

1. Before you light the candle, scribe the address of the house into the side. Then using the key, press an imprint of the key into the side of the candle.
2. Place the candle in the middle of your table or altar. Light it.
3. Taking the keys, hold them above the flame (not so close as to burn them, and say:
   *May this key unlock the door to happiness.*
   *May this key unlock the door to health.*
   *May this key unlock the door to love.*
   *May this key unlock the door to wealth.*
4. Blow out the candle and say: *Blessed Be.*

The keys are now ready to be handed over to the new owners. And my keys are now ready to open the door to my new home, as well.

# Moving Protection

MOVING IS TRAUMATIC under the best of circumstances. There is the packing, deciding what to toss, what to keep, how you will move, when, and then actually getting to the new place and settling in. I like to bag up a little protection for the move.

THINGS YOU WILL NEED:
- Small draw-string cloth bag, either made or purchased, but should be of cotton, burlap, or silk
- One tablespoon of each of the following:
  Borage: courage
  Basil: protection and wealth
  Sage: wisdom
  Anise: purify and protect
  Coriander: to heal the sense of loss
  Sea salt: purify and protect
- Bowl

Time: New moon phase, but early Sunday morning is best

1. Gather all your herbs, and place them one by one in your bowl. Starting with sea salt, say: *I add sea salt to protect this endeavor and keep my heart pure.*
2. Then, add each of the ingredients, saying:
   *Borage to bring me courage.*
   *Sage to bring me wisdom.*
   *Basil, to protect me and give me wealth.*
   *Coriander to heal the sense of loss.*
   *Anise, to protect and purify.*
3. Mix the ingredients in the bowl, then pour them into the bag.
4. Seal the bag shut and thank the God and Goddess for their unwavering support. Finish with: *Blessed Be.*

If this is a long distance move, you will want to make sure that everyone involved is protected—including those that may not believe in the craft. Make sure to carry the protection bag on your person throughout the move and unpacking. I always place it in my left pocket. I make protection bags for everyone that helps me move. This is also a wonderful protection spell for general traveling.

TIP: You can add other herbs based on their magical characteristics to individualize the protection and blessing for each person and each event.

# Leaving This Abode Behind Blessing

THIS HOUSE HAS BEEN the focus of your life, the central point of your energies and/or your family. It is important to pay homage to the abode that has sheltered you, given you hope. Everyone in the household needs to recognize this space and hope for the future.

Time: Anytime

1. Gather everyone living in the house together in the area you consider the heart of the home.
2. As a group, hold hands and say: *Welcome to the Circle.* To welcome the powers, everyone turns to the east. The east is the beginning, where the seed is formed. Each person needs to give thanks for the time you were in this house.
3. As a group, turn to the north, each person needs to say: *If I am ignorant of the right path, help show me. I give up whatever pain has been experienced in this place.*
4. As a group, turn to the south, each person giving thanks for the light and blessings of this house.
5. As a group turn to the west, asking that the powers help each person walk forth and gather the fruit of the days' labor.
6. Turning to face each other in a circle, say: *To all four directions, to all four winds in the swirl of life that have guided me here and there, good and bad, I thank you. Stay with me as I move on. Blessed Be.*

TIP: It is important that you leave behind bread and salt to welcome the new homeowners. This will ensure good tidings for them and continued good luck for you.

# Blessing for Your New Home

YOU MAY BE MOVING INTO a place that has been occupied before, it is important that you start fresh in a new home. You will need to banish the past. Before you move in the furniture, you need to clean "besom" the space. Buy or make a new broom (never, ever bring a used broom into your house), and while sweeping, say the following:

> *Out and down into the ground*
> *never rise again, again, again.*
> *Sweep clean, sweep clean,*
> *bring to me my favorite dream.*

You should also clean off all surfaces with a washing mixture of salt and rosemary. Rosemary is an especially welcoming herb. Remember to plant rosemary at your garden gate.

After you have cleaned, you may want to perform a Smudging Ceremony (see page ???) to clear the air and the spiritual space. I highly recommend performing the ceremony prior to moving in and occasionally throughout the year. If you are like me, I have a lot of people coming and going, and sometimes that bring in energies that I would rather not have in my living space.

## HOUSE BLESSING

This blessing may be used on both per-occupied houses and new construction. The ceremony not only blesses the space, but provides protection. It is best to perform the ceremony before you move in furniture and on the New Moon. But if that is not possible, it is still provides protection. Everyone that lives within the house should participate. You may also invite loved ones to share in the ritual.

THINGS YOU WILL NEED:
- Small table to use as an altar
- Three candles: Blue, Green, and Purple, cleansed and anointed
- Incense: either frankincense or sandlewood
- Two small bowls
- Salt water (preferably sea water)
- Three herbs: rose leaves for love, lavender for purification and happiness, and rosemary for protection and healing. You may add other herbs if there is an essential property you want to include.
- Bell
- Food and drink (red wine preferably)

Time: Anytime, but best on a New Moon

1. While you prepare for the ceremony, burn the incense on the altar.
2. Set the three candles on the table in a triangle shape. Put the most important candle for you, based on its properties and your own preferences, at the top of the point.

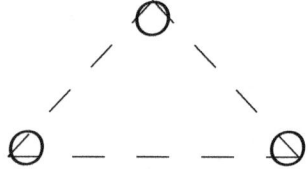

3. Have all participants sit before the candles. Each concentrate on the hopes and dreams you have for this new beginning. Light the candles, starting with the top one first, then the left, and finally the right.
4. Pour the salt water into one bowl.
5. Mix the herbs in the second bowl.
6. When everyone is calm and, say:
   *Hear us within. Hear us without.*
   *All that is negative, get out, out, out!*

7. Ring the bell three times, on each of the "outs."
8. Take the bowl with the salt water, and move the group outside. Move around the house in a counter-clockwise (widdershins) fashion, sprinkling the salt water about the exterior. Make sure to sprinkle water on each window and door.
9. Go back into the house the same door you exited. Taking the bowl of herbs, and move through the house in a clockwise (deosil) manner, sprinkling small amounts of herbs. You may invoke any deity you wish for protection of hearth and home.
10. Return to the altar. Repeat the above:
    *Hear us within. Hear us without.*
    *All that is negative, get out, out, out!*
11. Ring the bell three times on each of the "outs."
12. Blow out the candles, and say:
    *Blessed Be, Thank you for your intervention.*
13. Serve food and wine.
14. Remember to leave a little of the food and wine to take outside and return to the Earth.

# Closing the Circle

Hail to the West, Element of Water
We thank you for your watchful attendance. Go in Peace.

Hail to the South, Element of Fire
We thank you for your watchful attendance. Go in Peace.

Hail to the East, Element of Air
We thank you for your watchful attendance. Go in Peace.

Hail to the North, Element of Earth
We thank you for your watchful attendance. Go in Peace.

# The Circle is Now Closed

# Appendix

# List of Herbs, Plants & Gemstones

SAFETY TIP: *Not all herbs are appropriate to burn. It is important to not use toxic herbs, including some common cooking herbs. Some cooking herbs can omit harmful vapors. It is also important that you use herbs that have not be treated with pesticides or herbicides—these are also often harmful to burn.*

Some people believe it is best to grow their own herbs, and for most purposes I agree. But in the case of selling your house, that really isn't an option because you do not have enough time to start a new garden now. So it is better to buy the herbs themselves. If you have a local herb farm, I suggest you go there and get your fresh herbs. Herbs can also be purchased over the Internet. Usually, mail order herbs will come dried and per-cut, which will require you to make an incense burner blend, instead of a smudge stick, but they do work as well as the stick. Either way, it is important to buy organic to avoid the fumes caused by herbicides and pesticides.

TIP: If I am forced to use purchased herbs, I always cleanse them before use, to take away any negativity they have picked up in harvest, packaging, and shipping. For fresh herbs, I simply rinse in sea water. For dried herbs, I cleanse with smoke from patchouli incense.

**Internet Sites:**
Mountain Rose Herbs
    www.mountainroseherbs.com/candle/resins.html.
    My favorite online shop. Has burnables in bundles.
Blessed Maine Herbs
    www.blessedmaineherbs.com/sacredherbs.html.
    They also have pre made smudge sticks available.
Essential Dreams
    essencialdreams.com.
    More into medicinal herbs, but have a nice selection of mixtures.
    Website is a little difficult.
I&E Organics
    www.iandeorganics.com.
    Good section on smudging herbs.

Penn Herb Company, Ltd.
>www.pennherb.com.
>Great selection. Also great for essential oils.

Starwest Botanicals
>www.starwest-botanicals.com.
>Wonderful selection, but tend to be per-cut again.

Shining Mountain Herbs
>shiningmountainherbs.com.
>Have both fresh and dried herbs.

TIP: If you harvest and gather your own ingredients for a smudge stick, incense, or spell, it's customary to honor the gift from Nature by providing an offering and a short prayer. An offering can be any material, such as flour, cornmeal, or even candy should do just fine as long as the intent is the same. A short prayer, such as: *Thank you for granting us use of you and helping us with our work* is a nice way to acknowledge the plants' sacrifice and the gift from Nature.

## Herb, Plants, and Gemstone List:

**Adder's Tongue Fern,** *Ophioglossaceae*—Adder's Tongue is a small species of fern that is believed to have healing powers. It is part of the *Ophioglossaceae* family and is named because of its forked spikes. It is considered especially effective if gathered on a Waning Moon. It is also used in teas and ointments. When used in a smudging, it aids in the healing of bad energies.

**Alfalfa,** *Medicavo stiva*—Alfalfa brings in money and protects against financial misfortune. It is known for its anti-hunger properties. It is best when harvested at the Full Moon. Dry and burn in the cauldron and place ashes in a amulet for good financial luck.

**Almond,** *Prunus dulcis*—Almond or almond oil is known for its power to increase prosperity, wisdom, and success. It is a symbol of wakefulness to ancient Egyptians. It is primarily used as a carrier oil due to its lighter scent and texture used in money/success spells.

**Amber,** fossilized vegetable resin—Amber is associated with several long-observed beliefs, and is widely regarded as one of the luckiest gemstones. According to some legends, amber originated as the tears of the sisters of the dead Greek hero Meleager, and when worn, it would protect one from evil. It is also believed that amber will make a person or place more desirable, thus its use as part of a smudging, would make the place more desirable.

**Angelica**, *Angelica archangelica*—Associated with St. Michael the Archangel, angelica has many magical properties. Also called Root of the Holy Ghost, it is believed to protect against evil. Not commonly used in smudging, but is effective in other protection spells if the abode is believed to be haunted.

**Anise (Star Anise)**, *Pimpinella anisum*—also known as Anise Estrella, is considered good protection to ward off the evil eye. It is used to bring good luck in love, money, health, and prophetic dreaming. Some consider it a good aid to spiritual growth and clairvoyance when burned as incense. It is always best to use Anise on a New Moon.

**Ash**, *Fraxinus* species—The ash tree has always been of special importance among those trees and plants valued for their magical powers. Warning, it is considered a perilous act to damage an ash tree. The ash played a crucial role in the practices of ancient Greeks, Romans, and Norsemen. For the Norse, Yggdrail (the world tree) connects Heaven with Hell and is the source of the material from which the first man, Askr, was made. Not commonly used in a smudging ceremony, it is used especially when seeking love.

**Basil**, *Ocimum basilicum*—Basil represents fire and deity. It is known for bringing love and wealth, while offering protection. It is also used to provide courage. Some say it also works well for spells to enable flight. In business, many place basil at the bottom of cash drawers to bring in the dollars.

**Bayberry**, *Myrica pensylvanica*—Bayberry is known to bring prosperity and luck, especially when using the oil of the plant. The Druids believed that burning the leaves will enhance psychic powers and to produce visions. The bayberry can be an important addition to a smudging when preparing to sell a house. Write your wish to sell (timing and price) on a bay leaf and then burn it in the smudging to make your wish come true.

**Bay Laurel**, *Laurus nobilis*—The bay has been sacred since ancient times. In Rome, it was associated with Apollo and Aesculapius, the God of Medicine. It is commonly associated with victory, honor, and general good luck. It is also a good defense against evil. If used in smudging, it should be used very sparingly, due to the quality of the smoke and staying power of the odor.

**Bergamot**, *Monarda didyma*—Bergamot is associated with bringing prosperity. Fresh leaves are also rubbed onto money before spending it to ensure its return. Also used in "success" rituals and spells. The leaves of the orange bergamot should be slipped into the smudge bundle to attract money.

**Birch,** *Betula* spp.—Birch bark is a purifying or cleansing herb. It has been used heavily to exorcise spirits by gently striking possessed people or animals. It can be used in cleansing rites for spaces. Birch bark is also used for protection. It can be used in smudging to cleanse negative energy, but also in cleaning. Boil some of the bark in water, and then add this water to the bath, to cocoon yourself in protective energy or use as part of your cleaning solution.

**Blackberry,** *Rubus fructicosus*—Blackberries and blackberry leaves have been used to return evil to enemies. But in white magic, blackberry is used to invoke the Goddess to ask for protection, healing, and prosperity.

**Blueberry,** genus *Vaccinium*—Blueberries have long been known for their ability to protect the home. Keeping blueberries under the doormat will keep away undesirables. Eat blueberry pie when under attack. This gets the protection inside you and increases the herb's protectiveness. Adding blueberry stems or leaves to a smudging brings protection to the home, and when combined with "selling" spells, keeps undesirables away.

**Bracken,** *Pteridophyta* (fern)—These ferns have always been associated with protection against evil spirits. It is said that when a bracken stems that are cut, they appear to be the Greek letter *chi*, the first letter of Christ's name. Bracken spores are especially prized for their ability to bestow great power. But gathering the spores is difficult. It must be done before midnight on Midsummer's Eve and without letting one's hands touch the actual seeds. Not recommended for use in smudging unless it is believed that evil spirits are present.

**Buckwheat,** *Fagopyrum* spp.—This grain has amazing powers in attracting money and providing protection. It is perfect for any money spells, and a few grains in the corners of your kitchen pantry is said to ensure the residence of the home against poverty and starvation.

**Caraway,** *Carum carvi*—Known for its protective qualities, an object that holds some caraway seeds is theft free. It is also known for lust, health, and its ability to strengthen memory.

**Cedar,** genus *Cedrus*—The purification powers of cedar are revered in many cultures. Smoke of the cedar is purifying and also cures the predilection to having bad dreams. To heal head colds, place cedar upon the hot rocks in a sweat bath. A piece of cedar kept in the wallet or purse draws money. It can be burned to invoke Odin (the one-eyed deity of battle, magic, inspiration, and the dead). Using cedar bark or needles to a smudging is especially good if money is your goal—plus it just smells nice.

**Chicory,** *Cichorium intybus*—This blue-flowered plant has been the harbinger of good luck. It is also known to assist in overcoming obstacles of various kinds. For best results, chicory must be cut at noon or midnight on St. James' Day—July 25th—with a gold (or gold-colored) blade and in complete silence. Many people carry a small bit of chicory to promote frugality. If you anoint your body with chicory juice, you will obtain favors from great persons. It was once thought to make its possessors invisible and to open locked doors or boxes if held against the lock.

**Cinnamon,** *Cinnamomum zeylanicum*—This common household herb promotes dreaming, business success, healing, psychic powers, love, purification, protection, and spiritual growth. It is easy to understand why it is commonly used in spells and blessing to sell a house or bless a contract. Shopkeepers are known to sprinkle cinnamon on their front door-step to draw in trade. Gamblers are known to carry sachets of cinnamon to draw in luck and winnings.

**Clove,** *Eugenia caryophyliata*—This all around spice can be used for just about any magic. Many believe that burning cloves over a charcoal will increase prosperity. And cloves are often used in money drawing bags to be worn at times of contracts, gambling, or transporting money.

**Clover, White,** *Trifolium*—This common and unassuming herb is well known for its ability to cleanse. But it is also known for its ability to bring clarity of mind, protection, and love. It is also believed to break a jinx and put an end to crossed conditions. It is commonly used in smudging sticks and cleansing baths. Ceremonies using white clover are believed to be especially powerful and ridding bad energies.

**Coltsfoot,** *Tussilago farfara*—Coltsfoot is best known for its ability to promote love, peace, and tranquility. Its leaves has been used in love sachets and smoked to see visions of the future. In smudging, it is used to bring peace and harmony to the abode.

**Comfrey,** *Symphytum officinale*—Primarily used as a herbal medicine for healing winds, comfrey is also believed to have powers to bring good luck, especially when dealing with financial matters. When used in money and financial spells, use on the whole leave.

**Copal,** *Bereseru microphylla*—This is a powerful resin used in the same manor as amber. The Mayans used it as food for the gods. They believed that as the smoke of the copal would rise, it would carry their prayers to the ears of the gods. Copal is used in divination and in purification ceremonies. Copal is the frankincense of the Native American world.

**Coriander,** *Coriandrum sativum*—It is heavily used in love potions and spells. Supposedly adding powdered seeds to warm wine will create lust in the person who drinks it. It also has great powers for protection, especially of the home. Coriander is also used to heal, especially to mend differences between individuals.

**Dill,** *Anethum graveolens*—This common household herb is known for its protection against hexes and curses. But is also enhances magical knowledge, clarifies the mind, enhances psychic powers, as well as brings good luck and love. It is also good if used in health spells. Simply soak the seeds in water for three days and use the liquid in a bath to ward off disease.

**Dogwood,** genus *Cornus*—Dogwood's power lies in its ability to provide protection, keep secrets, and grant wishes. The lore of Appalachian culture says that to make a wish come true, collect three red dogwood berries, a dogwood leaf that has also turned red, and a few pieces of bark. Place all of these items on a piece of white fabric or in a pouch, and tie it up with red yarn. Speak words of power affirming your wish over this magic bundle. Pass the bundle above the flame of a red candle. Extinguish the candle and hide your magic bundle until you receive your wish. To increase the power of the dogwood, do the wish spell and add dogwood to your smudging bundle.

**Dragon's Blood,** *Daemomorops draco*—Dragon's Blood is a powerful herb used in many spells for love, protection, exorcism, and fertility. Many use it for magical inks. It is also used to entice old lovers to return when one burns the resin. It can be placed under the pillow to help guard against impotency. Many sprinkle it around homes for protection.

**Fennel,** *Foeniculum vulgare*—Used for confidence, strength, and courage, fennel is a great herb to include in any protection talisman. It also has properties of fertility and longevity. Other uses have included consecration, divination, energy, and meditation. It is a wonderful herb to include in any mid-summer ritual.

**Fir,** genus *Abies*—The fir tree or pine, with its evergreen foliage symbolizes such qualities as immortality and fertility. So when it is used in a smudging ceremony, it is used to promote fertility.

**Frankincense**, *Boswellia carteri*—This is an ancient herb used in the most magical traditions. The Egyptians believed it was sacred to the sun god Ra, and used it heavy in sacred rites of exorcism, purification, and protection. When burned as incense, it is known for its spirituality, aiding in love, consecration, blessings, energy, strength, healing, protection, and courage. It is also used in blessing and to purify ritual spaces.

**Galangal**, *Alpinia officinarum*—Galangal has the power of time perspective, so it is wonderful for astral travel. It is used primarily to aid in rituals to see the future, or to clarify some matter. It is also used for self-awareness.

**Garlic**, *Allium sativum*—Though best known in modern times as a safeguard against vampires, garlic has long been considered great protection against a number of evils. It's also great as a mosquito repellent. It is not often used in the smudging, simply due to the odor it leaves behind. It is better to use garlic cloves as a decoration, thus protecting from evil.

**Ginseng**, *Panax quinquefolius* and *P. schinseng*—Also known as Sang Root and Wonder of the World, ginseng is used primarily in sexual charms. But it also gives an emotional sensuality to abodes. To help control how others see the environment, many dust a little ginseng in the corners of the house for nine days to bring beauty and light to the space.

**Goldenrod**, *Solidago*—Ancient legend has it that good fortune comes to those who understand the workings of the goldenrod. To see your future love, wear a piece of goldenrod. He or she will appear on the morrow. When held in the hand, the flower nods in the direction of hidden or lost objects, or where buried treasure lies. If goldenrod springs up suddenly near the house door, unexpected good fortune will soon rain upon the family living there. Goldenrod is also used in money spells. Used when smudging for a house sale, it is believed that good buyers with good money will come to the door.

**Grass**, genus *Poaceae*—Many grasses are believed to have the power to bring good fortune in all money matters.

**Hazel**, genus *Corylopsis*—Hazel has been an effective defense against evil spirits and dark witchcraft, as well as a bringer of good luck. A forked hazel twig is especially favored. Harvested on the Full Moon. Because of its rarity, it is not often used in smudging.

**Heather,** *Calluna vulgaris*—Whether it is white or purple, heather brings good luck. It is quite common for drivers to stick a sprig of white heather in the grill of their car radiator to protect their fortune or for gypsies to sell sprigs of it for good luck. It can be used in smudging to bring luck, but is more commonly used in a potpourri or in a dried twig arrangement for good luck.

**Holly,** *Aquifoliaceae* species—Holly is known for its protective powers. Hanging holly in the house protects all within from evil witchcraft and other misfortunes. It is said the holly must be picked before Christmas Eve, but not taken into the house until Christmas Day. The prickly male variety is particularly lucky for men while the smooth-leaved female version is luck for women. It is not recommended to actually burn holly in a smudging, but if you are selling your home in winter, it is definitely a good idea to hang some holly for good luck. Holly is also used in the making of wands, especially for those in the craft that wish to spin a different truth.

**Jasmine,** genus *Jasminum*—This fragrant herb is believed to enhance love spells and lunar magic. Jasmine was grown in Egyptian temple gardens for beauty and to provide protection and longevity. It is an all around herb to be included in many kinds of spells. It is associated with compassion, dreams, family, fertility, gardening, healing, love, peace, promoting sleep, prophecy, prophetic dreaming, psychic awareness, sleep, and spirituality. It can be substituted for rosemary in most spells. Plus it just smells lovely when burned as incense, while bringing harmony to the space.

**Juniper,** genus *Juniperus*—Throughout the world, juniper is believed to have protective powers. Foxes and hares frequently use outcrops of Juniper as shelter when hunted. Juniper smoke will ward off evil spirits and disease, and will safeguard all those that reside within. It is an excellent plant to be included in a smudging bundle.

**Lavender,** *Lavandula*—Lavender holds special powers of bringing peace and balance to its surrounding area. When lavender is strewn into bonfires at Midsummer as an offering to the deities, it will bring peace, love, joy, and healing. Often used to induce sleep and relieve stress, lavender is a perfect addition to any smudging bundle. Its aroma is wonderful in the home and welcomes guests. When burned for purification, it frees emotional stress, brings inner calm, restores balance, and gives increased awareness. Lavender is one of the best herbs for a smudging bundle used in a house cleansing ceremony—and one I highly recommend.

**Licorice Root,** *Glycyrrhiza glabra*—Licorice root is used to take control over a place or situation. It is said that sprinkling licorice root around a room where you will meet someone for business, you will have the upper hand. This is not necessarily one of my favorites, but many swear by it.

**Mandrake,** *Mandragora,* genus *Atropa* (European) or *Podophyllum* (North America)—Mandrake has been used in old European witchcraft from ancient times. The man-like root is said to scream when pulled from the earth, and hearing its cries to portend death. At one time harvesters employed dogs to yank the mandrakes from the soil. It is primarily used in protection spells for home and business blessings. It is also known to bring good luck, prosperity, and protection. On the other side, it is known for use in exorcisms and divinations. It is always wise to be careful when using mandrake and any way other than prescribed by an experienced practicer of the craft.

**Marjoram** (sweet), *Origanum majorana*—This wonderful herb is great for cooking as well as magical spells. Its ability to heal and bring happiness makes it perfect for any culinary endeavor. It is also known for its ability to promote general health, bring prosperity, and encourage love.

**Meadowsweet,** *Filipendula ulmaria*—According to tradition, meadow-sweet is one of the Druid's most sacred herbs along with water mint and vervain. Its magic powers are love, divination, peace, and happiness. Meadowsweet was also one of the plants used in the creation of Bloddeuwedd 'Flower Face', wife of Lleu Llaw Gyffes (warrior and magician). It is traditional to include meadowsweet in bridal bouquets as it brings joy and blessings to the new bride. Anointing oneself and breathing in meadowsweet oil on Beltane eve is said to help one meet true love. I highly recommend using it in a smudge bundle. Use the leaves and bark, it brings love and harmony to the home.

**Mullein,** *Verbascum thapsus*—Mullein is known for its ability to chase away nightmares and engender courage. When it is burned, it chases away enemies. It has been used in the dark arts, so I believe mullein leaves and bark should be used with great caution.

**Mugwort,** *Atemesia vulgarus*—Primarily used to stimulate psychic awareness and prophetic dreams, mugwort is often used to chase away "bad spirits" by making them sick. Not recommended for smudge sticks unless you believe evil spirits are around.

**Myrrh,** *Commiphora myrrha*—Known throughout the ages as sacred to Isis, myrrh is a powerful herb. When used as an incense, it purifies and brings the ability to meditate in a peaceful environment. The smoke of myrrh is used often to consecrate, bless, and purify talismans, charms, and magic tools. It also guards against evil, promotes healing, and provides protection.

**Myrtle,** genus *Myrtaceae*—This simple evergreen shrub is lucky and is associated with love, marriage, and fertility. It is also known to promote peace and happiness of the household. It is better to plant a shrub on each side of the front door, but can be used in smudging, if it cannot be planted. Note, that the smoke can produce a strong odor, so use very sparingly.

**Nettle,** genus *Urtica*—Also known as "stinging weed," nettle is reputed to have the power to ward off lightning (not a bad thing for a house) and to bring courage to those in danger (again, not a bad thing when selling a house). Not to be used in a smudging bundle.

**Nutmeg,** *Myristica fragrans*—This spice producing plant has many luck-giving properties. Sprinkling the spice on the house sell-sheet will increase the chances of a good sale in quick order. Using a little nutmeg in smudging will also aid in good luck on a good sale. One should recite the address, date of sale, and price wanted (not necessarily the offering price), as one smudges.

**Oak** (white oak bark), *Quercus alba*—There is an old tradition, dating from the Druids that states one should embrace the tree within a sacred grove to get answers to questions previously not answered. Wands of potent magic are made of oak. It protects, encourages wealth, and luck.

**Oats,** *Avena sativa*—There are many that feel oats is primarily used for money spells. But it's medicinal uses make it very good for energy tonics and sexual endurance potions.

**Olive,** *Olea europaea*—The long-lived olive tree, mostly grown in the Mediterranean, has powers to bring peace, prosperity, beauty, and other positive qualities. It can be used in smudging, but is difficult to get and the smoke odor tends to linger longer than one would like for a home for sale—could be used more effectively in an outdoor smudging.

**Patchouli,** *Pogostemon patchouli* or *heyeanus*—Patchouli has many uses. It is known for its use in fertility talismans and can be substituted for "graveyard dust" in a number of spells. Patchouli smells like rich earth, so it is perfect for spells in selling house, because of its ability to attract money and buyers. It is also good for protection and purification.

**Peach,** *Prunus persica*—Chinese lore gives the peach an exalted place, as a symbol of long life and immortality, as well as the power to ward off evil. In Western culture, it is good luck. Peach twigs make an excellent addition to a simple smudging bundle.

**Pine,** genus *Pinus*—Pine is the all around spiritual cleanser. Now you understand why so many cleaning products tout the wonders of pine in their formulas. The Iroquois burned pine wood chips, needles, or resin as an incense when moving into a vacant house to drive out unwanted spirits. Putting pine needles in a bath will remove mental negativity. Its primary benefits include protection, purification, cleansing, prosperity, inner strength, healing, fertility, and success. It is a favorite in home and business cleansings and blessings. One little side benefit to pine is its ability to bring the user back down to earth in business and financial dealings.

**Poppy Seed,** *Papaver* species and *Somniferum*—Poppy seeds have been found in ancient tombs and archeological digs. The oldest written record of poppy was found in scrolls and art of Sumerian origin dating to around 3000 B.C. In magic, it is primarily used for fertility, fortune, and love. It is used in money and love charms, but is also beneficial in legal matters.

**Quartz,** crystal—This crystal is known for its ability to release one from the past and allow that person to move on to their future. It amplifies and transforms energy, so it is a powerful tool for both healing and magical purposes. It is know for its ability to increase the power of most spells and is excellent as an aid in recharging other stones and increasing the potency of herbs.

**Rose,** genus *Rosa*—Generally believed to be the symbol of love, it is also used to enhance attraction to places and things. Rose petals are used to increase the attractiveness of people, places, and items—allowing one to overlook simple flaws.

**Rosemary,** *Rosmarinus officinalis*—Rosemary is one of the most sacred of herbs. If drank in wine by newly-weds at their wedding breakfast, it is said the couple will be faithful in love. It also wards off the evil eye, can cure madness, guards against nightmares, and prevents storms. It is also used heavily in spells to reveal the future.

**Rue,** *Ruta graveolens*—"Rue" comes from Greek Reuo meaning to set free, because rue was consider highly effective at treating various diseases. Known for its healing and protection qualities, it is an excellent for house blessings and protection. It is also known to bring good fortune and luck to those that reside within the house. It's also good protection for those that make frequent astral journeys.

**Sage,** *Salvia*—Sage is prized for its ability to bring luck. Legend has it that it was introduced to the British Isles by the Romans, who dropped bits of it while marching along the roads they constructed. Sage promotes wisdom and improves memory, keeps spirits at bay, and brings harmony. White sage is most common in Native American smudging, promoting purity. Sage tends to be the foundation of any smudging.

- **Desert Sage,** *Artemesia tridentate*—This sage is known to drive out negative energies, spirits, and influences. It is an important part of a smudging for people and places before any sacred ceremony.
- **White Sage,** *Salvia apiana*—This sage can be used as any of the sages, but it is often preferred because it has a sweeter aroma. There is a simple purity to white sage.

**Sandlewood,** *Santalum album*—Used for consecration, immortality, and as a funeral herb. It has the capability to enhance visions. It can be used as a purifying incense. Not a good choice for smudging.

**Slippery Elm,** *Ulmus rubra*—Primarily a soothing herb, it is good for medications. It does have one interesting characteristic: if you wrap a yellow ribbon around it and throw into a fire, any gossip circulating about you will stop. There are those that believe that slippery elm also has persuasive properties.

**Sunflower,** *Helianthus annuus*—With its bright face of gold, following the sun through the sky each day, the sunflower brings wisdom, health, fertility, and happiness. It is believed that wishes are granted when sunflowers are involved. Sunflower leaves makes a wonderful addition to any cleansing smudge bundle.

**Sweet Clover,** *Melilotus officinalis*—Clover is one of the oldest cultivated plants. It has been used magically since ancient times. Although modern folklore has this three-leaved plant associated with the Christian Holy Trinity, the association of plants with three leaves goes much further back into Pagan times. The ancient Greeks and Romans associated it with their triple Goddesses and the Celts considered it a sacred symbol of the Sun. In folk magic sweet clover is used in a ritual bath to attract money and prosperity to the bather and is also used as a floor wash to chase out evil and unwanted ghosts.

**Sweetgrass,** *Hierochloe odorata*—Like sage, sweetgrass is a powerful cleanser and protector. It carries a powerful female energy. I keep a sweetgrass braid over my door to keep positive energy flowing in my home. Sweetgrass is also very popular for smudging.

**Tansy,** *Tanacetum vulgare*—Tansy is known for its properties of immortality and longevity. Once used as part of embalming preparations, today branches are used in aspersing a body, a grave site, or a ritual area. Tansy's association with rebirth is strong, that is the reason it is often used in cleansing ceremonies.

**Tulip,** genus *Tulipa*—Because tulips have a number of different magical associations and they are so easily available, they are used in a vast array of spells and blessings for a number of purposes. Planting the bulbs (of different colors) will attract good luck and, friends, lovers, and financial well-being to the house and those who reside there. The various colors of tulips add to spells: purple for Full Moon workings related to love magic; Orange for attraction and encouragement; yellow near your door or under your windowsill protects; white is for purity and cleansing.

**Turmeric** (root), *Curcuma longa*—Most people know turmeric for its use in Indian food, but is has the magic of passion. It commands confidence, courage, and strength—both of mind and body. Has been used for exorcisms and for breaking spells.

**Uva Ursi,** *Arctostaphylos uva ursi*—The uva ursi, or common bearberry, is considered a magical plant whose powers included protection against ghosts. Its name refers to the bears' fondness for the plant's red fruit; *uva-ursi* means "bear's grape" in Latin. It is used in smudge bundles specifically if ghosts are believed to be present.

**Valerian,** *Valeriana officinalis*—Most know this herb for its medicinal qualities as a sleep and calming agent. Its magic properties include love, purification, and protection. It is often used in spells and potions to reunite fighting couples or family. It's ability to bring harmony makes it a good household herb.

**Vervain,** *Verbena hastata*—A herb of the verbena family, blue vervain is accredited with many magical powers. The Druids venerated the plant for its qualities, and it continues to be of importance to herbalists and Wicca today—sometimes dubbed the "enchanter's plant." It is know to ward off evil and ensure prosperity of the occupants. It is also known to be used on love potions.

**Willow,** genus *Salix*—The willow has long been associated with sorrow and lost love. In past times, it was customary for a person in mourning to wear sprigs of willow to indicate their loss. Willow also wards off evil and brings luck when burned. It is believed that by burning the bark and/or leaves of the willow, one burns the "sorrow"; thus, making willow a very good part of a smudging to prepare one to sell the house they have loved or to help relieve the despair of loss.

**Witch Hazel,** *Hamamelis virginicana*—The Native Americans were well acquainted with this exceptional medicinal plant initially found in Nova Scotia and Ontario, as well as south Texas and Florida. The liquid from the plant is a natural astringent, and the bark and leaves contain large amounts of tannins. In magic, witch hazel is primarily used for protection and healing of the heart.

**Yarrow,** *Achillea millefolium*—Yarrow is also known as "soldier's woundwort" and provides protection. Yarrow is also used to exorcise evil and negativity from a person, place, or thing. Legend has it that yarrow was the first herb that the infant Jesus held in his small hand. It is also holds powers to keep all offers true—whether that is a lover or possibly a buyer. This makes a very good addition to any smudging for selling a house.

# Selling a Haunted House

Selling a haunted house can be potentially problematic—or a blessing. Believe it or not, there are buyers out there that are specifically looking to buy a haunted house. Generally, speaking though, haunted houses take longer to sell.

My brother purchased a haunted plantation in Missouri. The farm dated back to the early 1830s, and had a great deal of historical value. It was well-known around the area that Miranda (the first mistress of the home and mother of thirteen) haunted the house and surrounding gardens. And the original slave quarters were also said to be haunted. All the residing spirits were known to be generally friendly, although Miranda had a habit of taking small items, such as keys, and hiding them. The ghosts were a bonus as far as my brother was concerned.

Upon moving into the house, my brother and his wife, had a formal meeting to introduce themselves to the spirits and set down ground rules for their time together. Specifically, they asked that all the ghosts stay outside the main house, with the exception of Miranda. She was instructed that she was not to touch the antique porcelain collection and that house and car keys were to be left alone. The property has been a place of contentment for all parties for over fifteen years.

### Is The Haunted House?

The first thing is to make sure the house is really haunted. Many people believe a place is haunted, but in reality it is nothing or just residual energy. Have you had personal experiences in the house that make you believe it is haunted? Does the house have a history of haunting? If in doubt, call in the experts. You can find legitimate ghost hunters on the Internet. Look for teams doing research in the paranormal. They can provide research on the history on the property.

Symptoms of a Haunting:
- Objects disappearing and reappearing in the house, or un-identified objects appearing.
- Hear sounds of voices, walking, doors closing, laughter, or crying.
- Lights and other appliances going on and off on their own. (Make sure to have an electrician check this out for safety.)
- Finding unexplained markings in the house, such as scratches or dark symbols.

- Feeling a presence in the house, the feeling of being "watched."
- Seeing apparitions, unexplained shadows, or orbs.
- Pets whining or barking without explanations or unexpected death of a family pet.
- Frequent, unexplained illnesses in the house.
- Plants dying.
- Being touched when no one is in the room.
- Moving or levitating objects.
- Unexplained series of nightmares, especially with children.
- Unexplained cold spots.

**To Disclose or Not to Disclose:**

If the house is haunted, a decision regarding whether to disclosure this information about the property is critical. Generally speaking, if a seller knows something about a property and fails to disclose it, they are setting themselves up for a possible lawsuit. Being up-front about the hauntings and ghoulish histories is the best moral policy.

In many states, there are specific laws regarding the information you must provide to a potential buyer. Some of these laws include the disclosure of a death that has occurred on the property—sometimes there are time limits on this information, such as three years. Other states have specific laws regarding "haunted" properties. Some of the states include: California, Colorado, Connecticut, Delaware, Florida, Georgia, Hawaii, Idaho, Kentucky, Louisiana, Maryland, Missouri, New Mexico, Oklahoma, Oregon, Rhode Island, South Carolina, South Dakota, Texas, Utah, and Virginia. Some other states have laws regarding "stigmatized" property—that is property where there are rumored hauntings. If you have questions, it is best to discuss the situation with your realtor, or if you are acting as your own agent, discuss it with a real estate attorney.

I currently have a poltergeist around the house. I hate to describe it as a "ghost," because I do not believe that it is the spirit of a deceased individual. It tends to like to bang doors and call out family names in the middle of the night. This is somewhat disturbing, especially if you are in the middle of good REM sleep, but otherwise, it is completely harmless. But, when I go to sell this house, I will try to exorcise it, and if that doesn't work, I will disclose it to a new buyer. There is no sense in causing someone to panic.

# Practical Stuff Preparing to Sell

Preparing to sell your house is no easy task. Like it or not, you truly need to go through the process of preparing the house and yourself spiritually and physically. The reasons are threefold:

- You must create the right energies for a buyer to accept this place as their new home, and for the home to accept the new buyers.
- You need to prepare yourself for the separation from this place you have called home.
- And finally, you must first do everything humanly possible to accomplish the feat at hand, before asking for powerful intervention from higher powers.

## Every Home Has An Energy

So you've made the decision to sell. Have you really? It's more than the intellectual decision to sell for whatever reason. You must decide to let go of this familiar part of your life and step into the unknown—selling always means a move. Are you ready to move? Can you let go of this house? It isn't just positive emotions that bind us; negative emotions can be just as powerful, if not more powerful. Strong energy, negative or positive, binds the spirit to place. Sometimes it takes an energy equally strong as the old to make us walk into the new.

Let's walk through your home, and help you let go. Let's take this in slow steps. Do not start at whatever you consider to be the heart of the house or the place you've loved the most.

TIP: You will be trying to sense the energies of your own home. Since you are used to how the house feels, it is often a good idea to enhance the energies levels. Use amber as a way to enhance the energies. An amber bracelet should be worn with the amber touching the inside of the left wrist (closest to your pulse), a necklace should be long enough so that the amber touches the chest right above the hear, or hold a piece of raw amber in your left hand. See page ???.

**Negative Spaces**

Let's start with the room you've always felt a little hesitant about—

you've had mixed feelings. This does not mean you start in the room you've always hated and never wanted to go into. Start with the room that never had that much feeling attached to it, for whatever reason.

Obviously, this can be any room in your house. Only you know which room that is. (If there is no room in your house that is without strong feeling, skip this step.) Step into this room. Why have you never "connected" with it? (This process will help you find your new place to live). Was it the light? The shape of the room? Or did you never make it your own? If you didn't, why? If you have no conscious answer, just quietly seeking an understanding to the energies of the room.

Now let's move onto the negative room or rooms. If the home office has been a place of stress, always working late or on weekends, never catching up—pay special attention to this space. It may require a special cleansing and blessing. Is it the bedroom where you had too many stressed out fights with your mate? Is it the living room where you worried or fretted while watching television or tying to read?

You'll know this room. It's the one you don't want to walk into. To walk into a space means to leave one reality for another. Sometimes good, sometimes bad. Strong energy means something is still holding you in these spaces. You are the one who know which room or rooms these are. No one can tell you. Saying goodbye to this room means you're saying goodbye to that time in your life when you struggled all night to finish a report to meet a deadline, or argued with your mate about finances, or struggled with your children's problems. It happened. It's over now. You may think you can't wait to see the last of this room. You may think you'll never buy or rent a space that is anything like it again. Come to terms with the feelings in this room or, more likely than not, you'll bring the same feelings into your new space. We're all compulsive gamblers. We repeat and repeat, sure that this time we'll win.

If there is a room which harkens backs to a tragedy, that may require a special ritual. You may need to call in a professional to help, but try scrubbing the floors of the room with the spring water used to charge the crystal, then a rose crystal cleansing, and a smudging.

## Positive Spaces

Equally there may be a room that you always liked, loved to walk into and enjoyed each moment you spent there. It can also be the office room where you did your best work or had your most original ideas and always loved the way the light fell or the shadows played. It can be the bedroom where you and your mate found each other again and that stability kept it all going. It can be the children's rooms where you enjoyed their laughter and felt whole knowing they were safe there with you under the same room. It can be the dining room where you spent many happy meals with loved ones or by yourself. That room will never leave you just as a deep love never leaves us. But it is time to move on and allow that love to find expression in a new place. The love remains. Nothing physical (a house or finances) will ever change that. That is your strength. That is your spirit. You will still have it with you. Leaving the house does not mean you are leaving that, you are allowing it to find added expression and it will. But it is always hard to leave what we love. It is delusion to think that space can hold your soul unless the soul is willing.

Possibly a room has both, as life so often does—joy and despair, happiness and frustration, disappointment, and fulfillment.

If you've been walking through your house, feeling worried and frustrated about the unknown that lies ahead, you probably haven't really looked at the house in some time. You haven't removed your stressed-out self from the environment. Do you remember what you thought of the house when you first walked in? Was the house a disappointment or did it live up to your initial expectations? Whichever the result, it's now time to step back, and take a good look at this space.

Life is far stronger than a house or a financial condition; life will move forward and take you with it, as it has always done. Go with it in joy and you will begin to see what it is trying to teach you. Right now, it is saying it's time to move on. So let's move on. Not in resentment or worry or disappointment or frustration or a bitter memory of what was once yours and no longer is or what you hoped for that never materialized. You've learned in this house. Only you know what you've learned and if you can only laugh sarcastically and say "I've learned all right," you're not seeing past the delusion yet. And most likely you'll walk right into another delusion. If you bought the house too high, why did you? Ask yourself why you were so willing to believe the mania of the time. If you bought the house very low or inherited and not leap with joy at the probable profit, be careful this isn't the same greed that made people buy houses way past their income possibilities.

## Creating the Right Space

So, let's begin with the physical tasks of getting the house ready for sale. Basically, we are going to follow the tried-and-true recommendations of real estate professionals. This could take a week to ten days.

**Clean, Clean, Clean**—The first thing to do is a good cleaning—not a cleansing (that comes later). It is the time to get out the broom, mop, dust cloth, and vacuum. Start in one room and clean it before moving to the next. Make sure it is the most thorough cleaning possible. Clean floors, walls, sweep out cobwebs from the corners, dust furniture, and wash linen and curtains (if necessary). Wash the windows—inside and out.

If you have a fireplace, make sure to clean it thoroughly. Consider bringing in a professional chimney sweep to do the job. Not only will the chimney look great, but chimney sweeps carry very good energy.

In the kitchen, make sure to clean out all the cabinets and organize. You will also need to clean out the refrigerator, microwave, oven, and stove top. Wax the floors, too.

Bathrooms need to appear as if no one has ever used it before. So no soap in the shower, all the shampoo bottles need to disappear, clear out the clutter in the linen closet and the bathroom cabinets. Bleach dingy grout around the shower and tub. Bright colors should be avoided—think "retreat."

Often these days, we're not as aware of odor as previous generations were. They were not bombarded by chemicals on a daily basis. But odors are always there and always communicating with the subconscious, with our sense of well-being or dread, our desire to get closer or move on. This is often so subtle few even think of it because they're not aware of smelling anything. Modern life demands that we consciously block so many aromas, except the most extreme. But smells are being registered, good or bad—they are closest to our memory and subconscious. What smells do you enjoy? The smell of fresh flowers or incense? In making your choice do not go too extreme; as with color, your choice may not be another's. But be aware if there is a musky or slightly unpleasant odor in the house. If so, and you can find the source, clean it.

A pleasant, subtle smell always appeals. But don't be like the woman who puts on loud perfume demanding attention. Often the attention involves a certain repulsion. The fine perfumes are always subtle. The soft smell of citrus tends to remind everyone of a fresh, clean space.

The master bedroom is the place of power, honor, and protection. The bed should be furthermost from the door and facing the entry to the house. This room is one of serenity, relaxation, and romance. Paint it in soft tones of green, lavender, or blue. Avoid any sense of indecision or chaos in this room such as too much furniture, shabby rugs, or disheveled bed linen. Again, think oasis from the chaos.

Go outside and see how your house first impresses the prospective buyer. How does it say hello to a stranger? Does it say hi, but I'm tired and just got out of bed? Does it say, hello but I'd just as soon you didn't come one step closer. Does it shout hello and let me overpower you with my amazing personality. Rent a pressure washer and spray down sidewalks and the exterior of the house. Patios, yards, and gardens need to be completely cleared of old debris, and dying/dead plants.

As with the inside of the house, let the house speak its own message, the one that lured you. Keep the sidewalks clear. Mow the lawn. Trim the hedges. Make sure the buyer can clearly read your house number and isn't out in the car worried if it's the right house. Worry is no way to start a relationship. Plant yellow flowers in the front. Yellow is the life-giving sun. It says this is the bright new beginning. The exterior obviously and immediately telegraphs to the buyer your care of the house.

Don't forget the laundry room, basement, and, most importantly, the garage. Clean and organize. Show of the space.

While you clean, keep a notebook with you and write down all the extra little things you see that will need attention. Things like leaky faucets, burned out light bulbs, and squeaky hinges are not only annoying, they create bad energies in the house. It is important that you go back and do all the basic repairs, as well. Replace cracked floor or counter tiles, patch holes in walls, fix broken drawers, etc. Not only will the house show better to a potential buyer, it will improve the energy of the house.

If you have a favorite item such a chandelier or door knocker that you do not intend to sell with the house, take it down before opening the house to buyers. Don't promise them something you're not going to delivery. It's deception, even if by oversight. It can cool any sale. Replace with new, appropriate items of good quality.

De-Clutter—It is absolutely amazing how much "stuff" we all collect. All this "stuff" just weighs us down, and it will "weigh down" a potential buyer's decision to buy, as well. So, now is the time to throw it away, donate it, or pack it away for the new house. Go room-by-room and remove all the extra "stuff" of your life in this house.

The basic rule is that if you have not used an item for at least one year, ask yourself, do you need it? This is a great start to the packing you are going to do when the house is sold. So as you box things up, consider what place this stuff holds in your life? Consider whether it enhances you living space, or detracts. Do you really want it in your new home? If the answer is no; then donate it, sell it, recycle it, or just throw it away. If the answer is yes, then begin packing. Make sure as you pack, that you are not just throwing things in a box, but securing the position for the actual transit to you new home.

What does a house hunter consider "clutter." It is all the stuff that gets in the way of the potential buyer's ability to see (actually feel) themselves in the home. So, you will need to pack-up all your knickknacks and special collections. Pack-up all those over-crowded bookshelves, leaving only a few tasteful books on the shelves with appropriate accessories. Clear off all the stuff on your kitchen counters—the general rule is two appliances on the counter (usually coffee-maker and toaster). In the bathroom, clear the counters.

You will also need to sort out your closets—keeping only the things you will be using in the next few weeks, and only seasonal clothes. This will make the closets look larger and show that the house does not lack space. It's human nature to be curious, so expect possible buyers to open drawers and look into closets. Who can resist? The buyer is facing unknowns and every peak will help settle the case, define the future. So go through your closets and throw out, store, and organize. Line up your shoes and if you have too many for the closet, maybe it's time to give some to those who may need shoes.

If you are overly attached to items in the house, just remember material objects are easily forgotten despite their hypnotic spell when you acquired them. They are shadow. A year from now you won't even remember what they were because ultimately they are not important.

Space is as important, if not more important, than things. Leave space so the buyer can see himself/herself in that space, can imagine a future there. He or she doesn't want to imagine your future.

**De-Personalize**—It's now time to really start to deal with your own energy in the house. While you will still be packing things away, this is the beginning of moving on with your life. Remember, it is now ab out the energy of the house, not the personality of the residents.

Go through the house and collect those personal items that marked this space as yours—photographs, family heirlooms, and knickknacks of whatever sort. This includes family photos or those of loved ones, prints or paintings that are particularly your taste, or have special meaning to you.

I have a collection of painting done my an artist friend. They are bold and speak directly to me and my relationship with the artists. But they are clearly my personal taste and are not easily understood by others. So, when I sell, these paintings immediately come down and are packed aware for the next home.

By removing these items, you're saying to the new buyer; this space is yours now. You're inviting the potential buyer in. People feel when someone is saying "stay away" even if that person consciously thinks they are saying the opposite. If you have particularly precious things, store them in a box in your closet or a safe place. Nobody wants to come to house and feel it is already possessed by another personality who most likely will be different. Personal items on display tell the buyer to stay away and the buyer will get the message.

If you are unsure that you have neutralized the "you" in the house, invite the realtor or a friend to come for a walk-through to evaluate the energy in the house.

If you have a personal spiritual alter in your home, it will be necessary to ritually dismantle it. You will need to explain to the ancestors and friendly spirits that you are selling this property, and that you ask their assistance in this endeavor. Further, you will need to explain that once the house has been sold, you will be moving to a new location and that the spirits and ancestors are welcome to join the move.

When you dismantle your alter, reserve one small item to hold from the altar to travel with you to your new home. This will allow the spirits to easily follow you and your energy.

Once you have cleaned, de-cluttered, and removed your personal stuff, the house is ready for the market and the blessings, spells, and rituals that will help you get the best possible results from the sale.